JOHN AND SUSAI

WINNING WITH HU

Illustrated by Christine Bousfield

J.A. ALLEN
London

First published in Great Britain by
J.A. Allen & Co. Ltd
1 Lower Grosvenor Place
London SW1W OEL
1989

British Library Cataloguing in Publication Data
Thorne, John
    Winning with hunter ponies.
    1. Livestock: ponies. Showing
    I. Title II. Thorne, Susan
    636.1'6

    ISBN 0-85131-473-2

Typeset by Rapid Communications Ltd, London WC1
Printed and bound by Bookcraft Ltd, Midsomer Norton, nr Bath, Avon

To
our children
and
their ponies

CONTENTS

PREFACE

This book is a joint effort; in some chapters we have co-operated, in others we have written individually. Not all the thoughts are original; we have discussed many aspects with our friends over many years, but our personal experiences have consolidated our knowledge from observation and study. If you recognise any of your wisdom in the book, we do not apologise, but acknowledge the influence of so many experts. However, our statements are backed by experience and we try to support them with sound reasons. We have produced ponies and riders for the show ring since our children were very young and now they have grown out of BSPS classes.

Having not been able to afford high prices for made ponies, we have had the experience of making our own. This has meant taking every opportunity to learn, and resulted in considerable success at the BSPS championships. Our ponies have often been placed in the open WHP classes; Longclose Spellbinder was placed seventh in his first year in the open 14 hh class; Catherston Telstar, who was 12.2 hh, was placed eleventh, tenth, ninth, seventh, and then fourth in the 13 hh class, to name but two talented ponies. Quarry Mill, a roan gelding, was chosen to go with the British team to Ireland in 1981. He was ridden by our daughter Victoria, and competed in both Northern and Southern Ireland, winning a strong hunter pony class in Dublin.

With these results in mind, we realise how much we have learned over the years, and understand the problems that newcomers to the showing scene may encounter.

We hope there are some useful chapters here for you to enjoy; no book answers all your questions, but we hope to stimulate your continuing interest to improve.

You may already have tried these classes with a pony, and have acquired a taste for showing as we did, and wish to take it more seriously; or you may be wanting to try them for the first time and are wondering what sort of pony to buy. Your rider may be a novice, or experienced, as may be your pony, but whatever your situation, we hope you will find something in these pages to help and encourage you.

Unlike many parents, we did not put our children straight into WHP classes. We encouraged a wide experience, which included hunter trials, eventing, dressage, mounted games, show-jumping, and especially hunting. We found that the WHP classes had much to offer us and soon realised that having the right type of pony was only a starting point. Much work had to be done by the rider, the trainer, and producer in order to achieve success. So showing became a useful exercise in character-building and family co-operation.

Working hunter pony classes are run under the rules of the British Show Pony Society in Great Britain, and under the rules of the Irish Pony Society in Ireland. These rules change from time to time, and what we have written relates to our understanding of the current position at the time of writing. You are advised to keep yourself up to date.

We have been regularly asked when we are going to print, so at long last we have put finger to computer; we appreciate all the friends who have encouraged us or who have had deep influences on our learning.

There are many people we would like to thank, and for varied reasons:

— our daughters Amelia and Victoria, for the years of fun we have all enjoyed together;

— the friends we have made at the shows;

— the people who encouraged Sue during her formative years – of these, three stand out as special:

— the late Joan Petty, who encouraged us so much when we first started showing, having produced herself the successful large hack Fantasy and the show hunter White Knight to be supreme champion at the Royal Show at Blackpool;

— the late Bess Gerard, who gave her guidance and endless opportunities to ride and hunt so many different and inter-esting horses;

— Eric Wright, so well known with the Quorn. A more gifted horseman one could not wish to meet, and a gentle person with a terrific sense of humour. He always had the answer on how to cope with a difficult or high-couraged horse. Add to this an ability to explain exactly what he meant to a child, and you have the perfect mentor;

—   Jacqueline Burton, a lifelong, knowledgable and mutual sounding board, for many hours of fascinating horse talk;

—   Geoffrey Warren TD, OBE, ex-chairman of BSPS Area 5, for his constant encouragement ('How's the book coming on?');

—   to Caroline Burt, of J.A. Allen & Co. Our thanks are due for her patience in guiding us through the many problems that occur when trying to put a book together;

—   to all who have lent photographs of their ponies;

—   to Christine Bousfield, for her brilliant illustrations which put into pictures what we were trying to say in words;

—   last, but not least, we thank Lesley Gowers for editing our book. It must have been a mammoth task for her and she took it all so effortlessly and courteously in her stride. She was able, with her vast experience, to put order into what must have been a maze of words.

Horses and ponies are a joy and a gift that we can enjoy throughout our lives; what a loss and a gap we would feel without them. We hope they and your children will help to fulfil your lives.

CHAPTER 1

Introducing the Hunter Pony

Relative to other types, the hunter pony is a newcomer to the show ring, although it has long existed for utilitarian purposes. The 1940s and 1950s saw the development of the show pony, with dedicated breeders concentrating on producing beautiful ponies for children to ride in the show ring. Many of these were a delight to watch and to ride, having good movement, presence and manners to match. Before this time show ponies were frequently accidents of nature and rather rare, usually crosses of small Thoroughbreds, Arabs and native breeds. By the 1960s as a result of years of careful breeding, they were consolidating into a definite type. At this time the improved economic climate encouraged a healthy demand for ponies to show. Also, gymkhanas and show-jumping were becoming more popular and good ponies were commanding very high prices. For this reason showing ponies tended to be a pursuit of the wealthy and those who owned show-pony studs. Amateur sportsmanship, as we understand the term, began to disappear, and professional producers swept the board. The time was ripe for change, and the working hunter pony was pony-showing's salvation, as well as the economic salvation of the British Show Pony Society. The advent of the WHP meant everyone could have a go, and everyone did. But the WHP had its own 'teething' problems and it was a while before the type was established. The first classes were full of failed show-jumpers, sub-standard show ponies and undisciplined family ponies.

In 1960 the BSPS invited a team of show ponies from America, and discovered that these ponies were expected to jump. A few years later it was decided to add an element of performance to some classes, and with great foresight the WHP classes were introduced. These had the familiar two phases: first, jumping round a course of rustic fences and, second, showing the pony in the manner of an adult working hunter class. These classes called for a pony of substance, jumping ability and soundness, and with good conformation, action, manners, temperament, quality and presence – quite a formidable set of requirements.

The heights of the ponies in the sections were selected to include 15 hh ponies for riders up to eighteen years. This had the advantage of easing children over sixteen years on to larger ponies and thereby bridging the gap between pony classes and adult classes. It also made the 14.2-15 hh pony more valuable; previously, unless he was dainty and well-trained enough to be a small hack, there was no job for a small horse/pony of this size in the show ring.

Since the advent of the WHP classes, the 14-15 hh pony has been very much in demand because there are now so many classes in which to show him.

The WHP has become a much sought-after pony in his own right. His popularity has gained momentum fast and his type has made a tremendous impact on the standard of the average children's riding pony. So long as our judges keep the true type in mind, he is likely to retain his characteristic temperament, performance, quality and presence, which are so highly prized.

In a relatively short space of time, since the first championship in 1968, the hunter pony has made a real impact on the ridden pony scene. He has probably contributed more to the pony world than any other type or breed before him.

Back in 1961, just a year after the American ponies came to England, Mrs Glenda Spooner put on classes for WHPs at the Ponies of Britain Show. Seven years later the BSPS put on their first WHP championship, which was organised by Mrs J. Gibson, Mrs D. Watchorn, Mrs J. Lee-Smith and Mrs M. Slattery. A total of sixty entries competed in three open WHP classes, and the show also provided unaffiliated show-jumping classes. Qualification for the championship was not required. By 1972 there were six classes, as the nursery stakes, first ridden and leading-rein classes were added. The show-jumping was dropped and ponies had to qualify for the three open WHP classes by being placed first or second in a qualifying class during the summer. The entries in each open class that year ranged from fifty-one to sixty-seven. From 1973 only winners at qualifying shows were eligible to compete at the championship. By 1986, there were thirty-six classes at the championships, fifteen of which were for WHPs or SHPs and there were an average of 111 entries in each of the open WHP classes, all of whom had to qualify by winning a class at an affiliated show.

The 1987 and 1988 championships included thirty-nine classes; this will increase in 1989 with the introduction of 15.2 hh classes.

HUNTER PONIES AND THE CHANGING SCENE

Since we first started writing, back in 1978, the showing scene has developed apace. Then the idea of showing ponies of the hunter type as a ridden class, without a jumping phase, was almost unheard of, except perhaps in Ireland.

The BSPS introduced experimental classes in their 1983 championships schedule and the show committee was overwhelmed by the response, there being about 130 entries in each of the three height classes.

These were repeated in 1984, with provisional rules being incorporated in the 1984 Year Book. The Royal International

Beckfield Ben Hur, owned by Mrs E. Barham, the first WHP supreme champion in 1968 and an all-round performer.

Rookery Jigsaw, owned by Mrs Flack, supreme winner in 1977 and another pony who won in many spheres. (Photo: Peter Rollinson)

Horse Show introduced show hunter ponies in 1984 and working hunter ponies in 1985, and qualifying classes were held throughout the country, mostly at BSPS area shows. Furthermore, the BSPS council later agreed that these classes be designated 'Show Hunter Ponies'.

These exciting developments helped establish these ponies as an entirely separate type, to the ultimate benefit of both the show pony and the hunter pony. Judges are now expected to distinguish two different types. In 1984, for the first time, the two were described in the BSPS Year Book.

Looking to the future we can expect further classes to be provided for hunter-type ponies. For some years the Ponies of Britain and the National Pony Society have included classes for WHP youngstock at their shows; we believe that classes of this type will spread to more shows.

A pony will be able to move in a natural progression through the show classes provided, being shown in hunter pony youngstock classes from a foal to three years; in novice show hunter pony classes as a four-year-old; in novice WHP classes in the winter season as a four- to five-year-old; then in open SHP and WHP classes at five or six years.

It is hoped that they will be hunted, hunter trialed, Pony Club evented, perhaps ridden under side-saddle, take part in dressage competitions and engage in many other activities to complete their education. When they are fully mature, both physically and mentally, and experienced, they are ready for the open WHP classes at the BSPS championships, which is seen as the ultimate test.

A recent development is an extension of the age group for riders in BSPS classes up to and including twenty-one years with the introduction of classes for 'Associates'. These include WHP and SHP classes. They have been introduced to close a gap between children's and adult classes, the adult societies not having had much success in fulfilling this need. The next progression will be the inclusion of 15.2 hh horses.

It is interesting to see how these associate classes are developing. So far, they are indeed proving their worth and classes at the championship show are very well supported.

In 1985 the Hunter Pony Stud Book Register was founded in order to encourage and establish the breeding of ponies of the true hunter type to a high standard. This is a register of winning ponies and others entered after inspection. Most are mares who have proved themselves in the show ring, many being of unknown breeding. The ponies coming forward for registration as winners of youngstock and breeding classes are mostly indigenous breeds crossed with other blood. Welsh Section 'A's and Dartmoors, crossed with tiny riding ponies, are producing the cradle and nursery stakes types. The 13 hh and 14 hh ponies are coming from Welsh Section 'A's and 'C's or New Forests crossed with Thoroughbreds, Arabs, Welsh Section 'B's and riding ponies. The 15 hh ponies are usually Thoroughbreds or Arabs crossed with Fells, Dales and Connemaras, and their progeny. Shetlands, Exmoors and Highlands seem to feature less in the breeding of the WHP type, but most WHPs do have some indigenous stock in their pedigree.

CHAPTER 2

Planning a Show Career

ESTABLISHING OBJECTIVES

Having become hooked on showing working hunter ponies, it becomes essential to plan out your showing career. You are much more likely to achieve success if you set about the task systematically. Your plan will depend on your motives, which need to be identified if you are to make the best of the opportunities open to your pony or ponies. If you aspire to reach the top, which we hope you will, make jolly sure that you enjoy the business of showing. Then if you do not succeed in your aims, at least you will have had an enjoyable and character-building episode for your children, as well as an interesting family hobby.

Let us consider the pony first. The pony you buy will depend on your ability to produce it, your jockey's competence as a rider and many other factors, including the depth of your pocket. You will therefore need to decide at what stage of a pony's career you are going to buy him and this will dictate the type of shows you enter.

If you already have a pony, you must assess him realistically and set your objectives accordingly. Conversely, if you do not have a pony, then you may decide to consider your objectives first and then look for an appropriate animal afterwards. Suitable objectives might be: initially qualifying your pony for the novice or open championships during the season and you may aspire to compete in one of the championships too; you might decide that the fun of competing as a member of a BSPS team at area or national level is a suitable ambition; or you might wish to qualify and compete at the Royal International Horse Show.

Establishing such objectives will bring structure to your showing activities. On the other hand, you may decide just to have fun and if this leads to any of the above, then that would be a bonus. But even this objective should be agreed amongst the

Catherston Telstar. Though only 12.2 hh, a superb show jumper and Pony Club eventer, with dressage scores below 20 points. (Photo: J. Thorne)

team beforehand to avoid disappointments, because each member will have different expectations.

Establishing objectives will enable you to decide which of the many shows and classes you should enter in the forthcoming season; decisions will be easier if you know what you want to achieve. Picking the right show for your ability level will give a good balance between challenge and success.

The season is a natural period over which to measure objectives but there is nothing to prevent you extending over many seasons.

No plan should become a straight-jacket; clearly things can go amiss, e.g. ponies have a habit of going lame just at the wrong moment. Be prepared to review progress and modify your ideas.

Novice championships

Your first objective could be to qualify for the novice championship at the end of the winter season. If you have an experienced, confident and tactful rider for your novice pony, the novice winter shows, usually held indoors, are an ideal environment for a youngster. They help him to concentrate on his work without being asked too many difficult questions in terms of fences to be jumped. There are novice classes at the open championship in the autumn and those who qualify in classes throughout the summer may compete.

The open championships

Your next objective could be the BSPS open championships in the autumn. The most prestigious classes at this show are the open WHP classes. A pony must win a class at a qualifying show to be eligible to compete. However, the whole spectrum of BSPS classes are catered for.

The open WHP classes need a very good and courageous pony ridden by a jockey who is experienced. It could be a mistake to enter these classes, even if you qualify, if you realise that either the pony or the jockey is not ready. To prepare for the championships it is a good idea to take part in some Pony Club events as these will give the pony a chance both to get really fit and to experience many and varied fences. The dressage will help to settle the pony and encourage a little discipline.

If you are looking for a pony to buy, the championship show is possibly the greatest opportunity you could have for seeing and comparing. If you find it difficult to evaluate a pony in isolation, then you should not miss the chance of seeing them all together at this show. You will be surprised what a difference it makes to your judgment.

A word of warning. Let us suppose that you have a good WHP and are enjoying a successful first season, perhaps qualifying several times and frequently being placed. If you have never been to the championships before, you may be in for a shock. With a class of well over a hundred qualified ponies in the same situation as yourself, the organisers have a daunting task to find the winner. Firstly, it would be no good their putting up half a dozen simple fences like those at your local show – that wouldn't sort out the best. You can expect at least a dozen, perhaps even fifteen, very solid fences. These might include several combinations, perhaps with three elements, a bounce, a ditch with water, a water jump like show-jumpers have, pens, changes of directions, walls and anything else that the coursebuilder can think up. Possibly there will be a total of between twenty and twenty-five actual fences to be jumped (see Fig. 13.2, page 173).

What is certain is that these jumps will be placed in such relative positions that only a rider in full control will be able to negotiate the course. The obstacles will appear in quick succession, allowing practically no time for a rider to recover from any minor *faux pas* before being confronted with the next challenging combination. This by itself wouldn't be too awesome, but there is also the electric atmosphere of the championship show to contend with.

People who show horses and ponies are competitive by definition. They tend to become rather tense on big occasions, not least parents ambitious for their children. This is quickly absorbed not only by the riders, but also by the ponies, who are sensitive creatures and seem to know that something important is happening. We have seen non-stoppers stop, usually fluent ponies go like unaffiliated show-jumpers, frequent falls and tears all round.

Van der Valk, owned by Mrs and the late Mr J. Massarella, won the supreme title in 1974. He was also a brilliant show jumper. (Photo: Peter Rollinson)

Longclose Hadleigh – a brave 14 hh open WHP, also a Pony Club team tetrathlon winner, bought and produced by the authors at four years.
(Photo: *J. Thorne*)

Ultimately the championship show is a test not just of a pony's ability but equally of how calmly and strategically the rider approaches a competition. A competitor who keeps his cool, walks the course intelligently, listens to useful advice, knows his pony well and learns quickly by other competitors' mistakes, will have a better chance of a good result.

However, having been warned of the difficulties that can be encountered, you may well ask, why then do so many exhibitors go? Because the championship has a special magic of its own. It is a real festival of all that is best in British ridden ponies, an occasion for hundreds of families to get together with one interest in common. It is the biggest show for ridden ponies in the world. It is really worth going to, even without your pony, just to let the children see all the ponies; you can also go through the catalogue and get the feel of the show. You will enjoy meeting other members at this social event. At present it is a three-day show with at least five rings in operation all the time; in every ring important classes and championships take place covering every aspect of the classes put on by the BSPS. Some of the classes – pairs, side-saddle,

Quarry Mill, produced by the authors. A brilliant WHP, silk-reined hunter and winner at Dublin. A pony well known for his sense of humour.
(Photo: *Carol Gilson*)

15 hh ridden pony class – do not have qualifying classes during the season, so any number may enter. The majority of the classes can only be entered if you have qualified by winning a class at an affiliated show. Read the schedule carefully as rules change from year to year.

Royal International Horse Show

This show is held in mid-summer and shows around the country have qualifying classes for both WHP and hunter ponies, so this is another show you may like to try qualifying for. It is, of course, a most important show and only ponies and riders who can cope with the tension of a big occasion ought to compete. It is currently (1988) held at the Birmingham Exhibition Centre, in July, and is run to a very strict timetable.

Teams – area and national

If you would like to be considered for a place in your BSPS area team then you should ask the appropriate person in your area if you may be considered. There is no harm in letting it be known that you are interested in being selected so long as you can take the disappointment if you do not make the grade.

Inter-area team showing is great fun and a very good way of meeting other families. Team competitions often take place at area shows but national teams are a different scene. Generally, ponies and children are watched at important shows throughout the year and are invited to be members of a national team. It is important that not only are the pony/rider combination winning regularly, but also their families need to be able to get on well with other people. Being a member of a national team is a fairly tense situation to be in and each family must therefore be able to cope with this and be courteous and kind when dealing with others also under stress.

PREPARATION AND TACTICS

As the main reasons for showing are fun and success, it may as well be admitted that the more success you have the more the family will enjoy it. Therefore, with this in mind, it is important to decide which types of show are the best ones for you to enter. If you have a very high-calibre pony and a good jockey to ride him then your aim will be the Royal shows, county shows and other prestigious shows and championships. If your pony is not of this quality it makes sense to compete at a different level, perhaps at riding club affiliated shows or hunt supporters' club shows. In between these two types will be found the BSPS area shows. However, it is worth sending off for as many schedules within your driving distance as possible; go through them carefully and choose what suits you best.

If your children are young try to avoid long journeys as these are very tiring for them; however, the shows which offer the qualifications you are striving for cannot all be on your doorstep. Some shows will offer several classes for your pony to enter, and this can be a bonus if you have one of these near enough for you to travel to. Take care when making your entries and keep a note of the classes you have entered. Make sure you keep the name and address of the secretary, which sometimes appears only on the entry form. Once this letter is posted the details may be difficult to come by.

Following a judge

You will quickly find that some judges like your type of pony more than others, so it makes sense to follow them where possible. There is no sense in knocking your head against a brick wall with a judge who obviously does not appreciate your pony. However, don't forget that you could be mistaken, or that a judge could find your pony 'grows' on him after seeing him more than once. You will have to use your discretion on this point.

TYPES OF SHOW

Royals

These are always highly organised, and the classes are kept to a very tight timetable. Parking will be restricted to a certain area and there may be delays getting on or off the showground owing to the large number of exhibitors and spectators. Nevertheless, these shows have an excitement of their own and are worth going to as soon as you are capable. Entries often have to be made many weeks ahead and entry fees are high. Prize money, however, is normally good.

County shows

These shows require entries well in advance, have high entry fees and are seldom the most sympathetic to the exhibitor. They are not always run by people who understand the needs of hunter ponies but, by the same token, these shows are prestigious, have good catalogues, and usually good prize money and trophies. Unfortunately, you often have to park a long way from the rings, and you may have to wait several hours to attend the grand parades. Generally, like Royal shows, these events are tiring to attend. The atmosphere is exciting, with crowds of people and possibly queues to get on to the ground. Plenty of time, therefore, needs to be allowed.

BSPS area shows

These are run by people who understand the requirements of the exhibitors and the best ones are often those which have a good representation of hunter pony people on their show committee. The schedules usually include all the BSPS classes, so there is plenty to enter; the entry money is not high, nor is the prize money, because these shows usually find it difficult to break even, let alone make a profit. They frequently have RIHS qualifiers.

Hunt supporters' club shows

These are usually well run, with interesting WHP courses and the judges are often genuine hunter judges. Entry fees are not high, nor is the prize money.

Riding club shows

These are very variable, often putting on BSPS classes as an experiment. They should be supported as much as possible to encourage more of them to include these classes.

CHAPTER 3

Management of the Hunter Pony

TEAMWORK

Producing a working pony with an effective jockey must be a team effort. A team might consist of at least a pony and rider plus a trainer or producer (perhaps this is Mum). There may be another pony and jockey in or outside the family. Dad may be added to the team as a driver. However big or small your team, make sure each person's responsibility is defined and leave him or her to perfect it. A golden rule: no raised voices, no cross words and no criticisms, only helpful comments and positive guidance. If there is ever an angry or critical word, nip it in the bud – it causes tension and limits progressive improvement.

Let's now look at some of the tasks to be allocated to your team members. Tack and clothes will need to be cleaned and set aside ready for the next show. Show documents, such as height certificates, membership cards, vaccination certificates, showground passes, etc. must be kept in order. Food must be prepared for the ponies travelling and for the people. Someone should co-ordinate the applications for show schedules and check that entries have been made at the correct time. Routes must be planned, the transport properly serviced at the right time and checked the day before the show for petrol, oil, etc.

One person must take responsibility for the training of the jockey and the pony. Obviously, it may be necessary to seek outside help on any points with which the pony or the child is having difficulty, but it is not a good idea to have two or three people helping in this area. Likely as not they won't all share the same views and this can confuse the jockey. Somebody must ensure that the pony is vaccinated and shod at the correct time, planning ahead so it is done in good time. Another person must take sole responsibility for the feeding, for this is a job for one person.

Ponies, like children, thrive on a well-ordered lifestyle, with regular meals, good food, quiet surroundings, comfortable beds, being at a comfortable temperature, plenty of work, and fun. A routine must be worked out to suit everyone and kept to as far as possible.

FACILITIES

You must look objectively at the facilities you have for looking after your pony and consider if they are adequate. If not, keeping the pony at livery may be the answer, or if someone outside the family is producing the pony, he may be kept at his or her yard. In this case the jockey must be able to travel to ride the pony regularly if they are to be successful. If your ponies are kept at home and looked after by the family, with or without the help of a groom, bear in mind that ponies seem to be collectable creatures. When a really nice one presents himself as a possible buy, it is handy to have a spare stable in which to accommodate him.

Your tack is probably best kept in the house if a purpose-built saddle room is not available. It should be stored in a dry, just warm atmosphere – too hot and the leather becomes hard and brittle, too cold and the leather becomes inflexible. Tack rooms attached to stable blocks are usually too cold and too far from the house to be thief-proof, so if you have a tack room like this it is probably best to use it for short feed, grooming kit, etc. If there is room, put in a sink and a tap as this makes life easier.

Rugs, i.e. stable and New Zealand rugs, can cause a storage problem. When not in use, clean and dry them and put them away carefully in sealed plastic bags. If in use but not actually being worn, a good way to store them is to hang them, tail end up, by two hooks on the wall. They will also dry well if hung in this way. Never leave rugs lying on the stable floor. If a suitable place does not present itself, hang a horizontal bar about 4 ft (1.2 m) long on a wall and fold the rugs over this. This works well so long as the pony is not a crib-biter or a playful fidget.

Whether your pony is shown off grass, or kept in, or a mixture of these, must depend on your routine, facilities, land, available help and how much work a pony has. Most ponies are not happy kept in a box twenty-four hours a day and, generally speaking, those that are ill-mannered, irritable or 'boil' unexpectedly are the ones who do not have enough freedom to graze, browse, roll, forage in the hedgrows and relax as nature intended.

Making your own hay is not worthwhile even if you have plenty of land. In fact, ponies are better off with hay from someone else's field, which will possibly give them a change of grasses and weeds; but, of course, you'll need somewhere dry to store it.

FEEDING

As stated, only one person should feed the pony. The reason for this is that only one person can really be familiar with what the pony is being fed and how well he is responding to his diet. If other people start feeding, no one knows what is happening. If any adjustments or supplementations need to be made then only the person who is responsible for feeding can make them. If this is understood from the outset, no one else need get involved. This person can also be in charge of working programmes, and it may be wise that he or she also deals with the vet and veterinary problems, keeping notes in a special book of the feeding details, veterinary treatments, farrier's visits, worming and teeth checking dates, etc.

Most experts will tell you to feed according to the size of animal and the amount of working he is doing. You must also consider the way he is managed, his temperament and the type of work he is doing. Showing is hard work, but it is not fast work. A show horse or pony needs to carry more weight and be well furnished but not fat. Equine athletes, like hunters, racehorses or eventers, need only to carry muscle and as little excess fat as possible, otherwise they put strain on the heart and lungs.

Most people, from our observations, go to one or other extreme. One sees hunters that are so thin at 'roughing-off' time, they could almost be called poor and in need of a good summer's rest to recover. But one also sees show ponies that are definitely too fat. Not sometimes, but often. This is a pity because it spoils their looks, alters their movement and hides their true conformation.

If you are feeding a horse for fast work, he needs lots of concentrated energy food, which is usually given in the form of oats, barley, maize, plus supplements of trace elements, minerals and vitamins, with a little high-quality hay. However, a show pony will need a very different diet. His frame should be well covered;

he should be healthy but not carrying too much flesh. Therefore his diet should consist of lower-energy foods, like sugar-beet, bran, carrots, supplements and the very best hay and grass – and plenty of fresh air. These foods can be given in proportions to suit the appetite and temperament of your show pony. We would advise giving oats only to a show animal who is too placid and shows no presence in the ring. Experiment with a little oats at first and keep trying until the correct proportions are found.

Ponies are very private eaters and must be left alone to eat undisturbed, otherwise they can become irritable in the stable. They are also fastidious creatures, so do keep their feed buckets scrupulously clean.

If you find your pony is difficult to feed and is too thin, or has a long frame to fill, you can try giving him some boiled food. Linseed given once a week works wonders and also helps the coat to shine. For each pony soak one cupful in a large pan of water and leave overnight. Next morning bring this to the boil and simmer for half an hour. Put it in a slow oven or warming drawer until the evening, when it can be added to bran and soaked sugar-beet. A little barley cooked in the same way will tempt a shy feeder. If you do not wish to go to the trouble of boiling barley, you can use ready-cooked flaked barley. This is just as good, but may not be quite so comforting to a tired pony as it isn't warm. Additional foods which add variety are carrots cut up lengthways, also apple, cabbage and parsnip peelings from the kitchen. Another feed useful for putting on weight is milk powder. Read the manufacturer's instructions and introduce it gradually in case the pony does not like it.

One of the best ways of getting the feed right for a pony is to ride him when only on hay or grass and feed him according to how he behaves. If he is good and calm you can gradually introduce short feed and increase this as his work progresses, never giving him more than the amount to keep him well, calm and obedient. This method avoids having an overfresh naughty pony.

Buy hay from a reputable hay-maker who takes a pride in his crop and does not include 'bonuses' such as ragwort and other dangerous weeds. If you trust him and always buy from him and pay promptly, he will look after you, even in lean years when hay of good quality may be more difficult to obtain.

Ragwort, a poisonous weed, is palatable to ponies when cut and dried because the percentage of sugar content rises; but there are toxins in the weed which irreparably damage the liver. Many sudden deaths from liver disease can be traced to ragwort poisoning (possibly with the previous owner). A good hay-maker will fertilise his land and allow his crop to grow; you will be able to see the hay standing before he cuts it and see the quality of the grasses. For ponies it is advantageous to have a few interesting weeds and flowers in the hay, as is usual in meadow hay.

Seed hay is a different proposition. It is very much harder, has a much coarser stalk and is frequently grown as a crop specifically for hunters, racehorses and horses in hard work. This is very suitable also for ponies but you will find that because it has a higher food value than meadow hay, less concentrated food will be needed.

New products are coming on the market all the time and one of these is Haylo. This is a grass feed which is half-way between hay and silage, and as such more of its nutritive content is available to the pony. The process bags the grass while it is moist, then excludes the air to preserve the goodness. It will keep for a very long time but is expensive to make, needing special equipment, so it is naturally more costly to buy. However, there is no waste and it is so nutritious. Again, less concentrates will be required, and as there is no dust, hay-dust allergy coughing will be a thing of the past. Many people soak hay before giving it to their pony, and this is certainly a good idea if he coughs, or as a precautionary measure when it is inclined to be dusty.

It is sensible to look well ahead and order fodder, hay and bedding in good time to avoid worrying about deliveries when there is snow on the ground and supplies are scarce. Remember that ponies have small stomachs and no pony should be expected to be put to bed at 4 p.m. in the winter and have to wait until 9 a.m. the following morning for his next meal and visit from you. It is too long.

WATERING

Water should be available to ponies at all times, all the year round. This can cause problems in the winter when everything freezes, and it can be hard work ensuring that enough is available. One way that can help is to feed sugar-beet pulp, making sure that it is really well soaked. When the weather is very cold, add a little warm water to the feeds, as much as the food will take. Not only will the extra liquid be appreciated, but the warmth also.

We have come across owners who have denied ponies water as a punishment. This is a very cruel and dangerous way to treat a pony, and could induce serious colic through impaction of the bowel.

If automatic drinkers are used, make sure they are cleaned frequently and double check that the mechanism is working, too.

STABLING AND BEDDING

The ideal size for a stable is, at least 12 ft by 12 ft (3.5 m by 3.5 m), bigger if possible. We have seen some extraordinary stabling arrangements, e.g. a low roof that continually kept the pony's head down; a low doorway, in what can only be described as a battery hutch; and others that are simply appalling. Try to have a high ceiling, a high and wide doorway, a window covered in mesh on the inside and two tie-rings. Do check the height of the bottom door: a little pony should not have to crane his neck to see over the top.

Whether you have a hay rack is a matter of choice but seeds can drop into the pony's eyes while he eats, and stretching up to reach hay can develop the muscles under the neck. A hay-net, or even putting hay into a manger or corner of the floor may be preferable.

In case your pony ever pulls away against his tie-rope, fix a short loop of binder twine on to the tie-rings and secure him to that instead of the rings. The loop will break easily and save a broken rope or headcollar.

Stables usually face south, but this can make them unbearably hot during the summer. Ours face east so they get the early morning sun. At the back of the stables is a high window for the afternoon sun to stream in. They all have centre drains, which undoubtedly keeps the bedding drier, and automatic drinkers.

Bedding must be a matter of choice. We have tried wheat straw, wood shavings and shredded paper, but have now settled with shavings, even though they tend to blow about the yard. We found that shredded paper became very soggy, soaking up the urine before it had a chance to drain away. Shavings or paper bedding can be a godsend to a pony who is allergic to straw and dust. Shredded

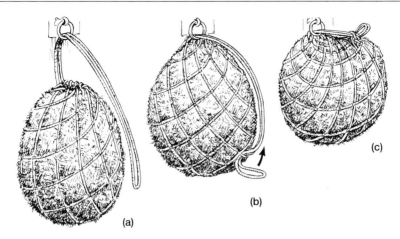

Fig. 3.1 How to tie up a hay-net safely. (a) Pull the net up to the top of the ring. (b) Put the end of the net rope through the base of the net and pull hard until level with the tie-ring. (c) Tie a quick-release knot at the top and tuck the long end of the rope into the net. Finally give the whole net a twizzle to secure it against the wall.

paper has proved itself to be particularly efficacious for this and many ponies have stopped coughing when bedded on it.

Increasingly, farmers have been spraying their crops with herbicides and pesticides, leaving poisonous residues on the straw. For this reason we no longer use straw in our yard. We now find shavings quick to muck out and once the bed has been established, it is not too expensive to keep up.

If you are lucky enough to have your own straw which has not been sprayed, then the best bedding to use is wheat straw. Oat straw is very tasty and the pony will eat it; barley straw has scratchy beards on it which will irritate the pony's skin, and can even get embedded like a splinter. If you constantly skep out the stable this will help to make the daily mucking out much easier.

Never be mean with bedding. It is important that it offers the pony plenty of protection from the floor: he will injure his hocks and elbows when he lies down and gets up if there is not enough bedding. Put plenty around the edge of the stable to avoid injury if the pony gets cast.

In the event that an animal is cast, do not panic. Talk to him quietly and try to get his head round towards the middle of the stable. If you have help, one of you should sit on his head while the other ties ropes to a leg. Get yourselves clear and gently encourage him to roll back over so that he can get up. If he had worn an anti-cast roller, he might not have got cast in the first place. However, most ponies do get up on their own if the head is moved to the centre of the box, allowing them room to get their legs under them to support their weight.

If there are any electrical sockets or light switches in the stable these will need to be covered so the pony cannot play with them. He could be electrocuted, so very great care needs to be taken.

If you have ponies who weave or crib-bite then you will have to take their problems into account. Ponies that weave stand with their legs slightly apart and sway their heads from side to side, usually over the stable door. Firstly, it is a very contagious habit, so other ponies in the yard will soon also be weaving; secondly, as they sway, they rock from leg to leg and this causes wear on the joints of the front legs. It is usually caused by boredom.

You can do two things: you can put a grille on the door so that the pony cannot sway over it, or place him in a box where other ponies cannot see him. However, this will add to his boredom problem if he cannot see other ponies, so try to place him so that he can see something that will keep him amused.

If he is a crib-biter, he will probably windsuck as well. He will arch his neck and swallow air, making a gulping noise, and he will probably hang on to something with his teeth at the same time. Everything graspable in sight will have to be removed from the stable, and a metal strip put over the top of the stable door to protect the woodwork. His habit will give him indigestion and he may be a poor doer, but on any account he must have a varied life to give him plenty to think about. Both these conditions are vices and often hereditary. I have seen foals windsucking on their mothers' hocks. Crib-biters wear down their teeth unevenly, so look out for this.

PADDOCKS

Whether you lease paddocks or have your own, it is well worth looking after them by keeping the fencing in good repair, removing all wire, and dividing them up so that they can be rested and fertilised in turn. A system of automatic drinking troughs with ball valves cuts down on work. A field shelter for each pony, and a field store for hay are much appreciated for those whose ponies live out. Try to harrow the paddocks thoroughly when it is dry enough in the spring, reseeding badly poached areas as the weather improves.

Bear in mind that ponies are gregarious creatures and hate living alone. If you only have one, try to borrow an old pony as company for yours.

If you have hedges don't be in too much of a hurry to have them trimmed. They offer excellent shelter and ponies love to browse them. Sometimes our ponies come in with purple lips, having been blackberrying. On one occasion our pony frightened a trespasser who dropped her basket of blackberries and fled. The pony ate all her blackberries!

If you have room, put a few cattle in with the ponies. They help to keep the paddocks well trimmed and will consume the horse worm eggs in the grass. As pony worms do not live inside cattle this is a very good way of keeping the paddock clean. They will also eat areas of grass which the ponies will not touch.

If your paddocks get particularly muddy your ponies may develop mud fever. This is like eczema and causes the skin at the back of the fetlocks to become inflamed. The hair must be cut away, the area thoroughly bathed and dried, and given a good application of pink heel ointment. (This is very like Germolene.) Keep a check on the heels every day until the skin clears. Mud fever can be a very painful condition, with the soreness extending up the front of the legs and even up to the underside of the stomach, so always be on the lookout for it.

Aim to have mares and geldings in separate fields to avoid squabbles, and arrange to put them out in even numbers. There is usually trouble with an odd one because ponies naturally pair off as 'buddies'. Avoid too many turned out together – rushing about in a gang can have obvious dangers of injuries and weight-loss.

THE COMBINED SYSTEM

This system entails keeping a pony partly in the stable and partly out at grass. It is a good system with advantages for both humans and equines and definitely helps keep the ponies sweet. We never keep a pony in for twenty-four hours a day, even when in work.

In winter we stable our ponies from 4 p.m. until 9 a.m. next morning. Then they go out, sometimes with plenty of rugs, and come in for tea at four o'clock. Having them in makes it easier for checking feet, injuries, feeding and generally keeping an eye on their health. They have bucket feeds at 5 p.m., 10 p.m. and 8 a.m., so there is no bickering over food in the field. They have access to hay, and a salt lick *ad lib* in the field.

This is a flexible system for it allows you to change the emphasis, if required, at any time without upsetting the pony. However, for children's ponies, even show animals, we feel it imperative they should go out as much as possible. To be out does not mean to be unfit. Ponies can walk miles in a field during the day, and since they will be ridden most days anyway, they could be fitter and more sane than ponies who are kept in.

Most small ponies can be kept out all the time in the summer, just bringing them in the night before a show. If you use this system watch the grass and look out for laminitis; and don't allow them to become fat. Fence off a small area of your field and use it as a slimming paddock.

GROOMING

Grooming is a very important part of a pony's life. In the natural state he would spend quite a while each day attending to his coat by rolling, nibbling and rubbing. When he rolls he digs the ground to make it rough and lowers himself with care into the prepared area. Some ponies are rather lazy and will use someone else's rolling place as it saves having to dig. A pony will often bite himself to try to remove loose hair, and if he cannot reach, will accept the help of another pony. We have all seen ponies biting each other across their withers, and although this is done as a recognition gesture, it certainly involves some mutual grooming.

In keeping a pony in captivity, we take him out of his natural surroundings, and must therefore be sure that we cater adequately for the very different life style he will live whilst in our care.

When your pony is brought in from the field, the first thing to do is to pick out his feet to remove caked mud and any stones that may lodge themselves near the frog or across the shoe. This must be done before and after exercise and is a good way of checking on the state of the pony's shoes and the health of the foot. While doing this feel the foot to see that it is cool, and be sure that there are no injuries in this region or anywhere on the legs. Finding and

Fig. 3.2 How to groom a pony safely. (a) Always face the pony's tail when grooming, then you will be aware if he intends to kick. (b) Use the hand nearest the pony.

treating injuries early on may save many days' lameness.

Brushing the pony helps to remove dirt, dust and loose hair from the coat and also stimulates the circulation. This in turn promotes a healthy skin and coat. Some of the grooming process can be done by hand. Ponies enjoy a massage just as we do, and much stiffness and aching can be relieved in this way. Treat your pony to a massage when you have a few moments. Using the fingers and ball of the thumb, gently massage the body, especially the muscles of the spine, shoulder, buttock and neck.

Wisping or thumping can be very good for him too, but be careful where you do it. Wherever you thump, the muscle will develop. Decide where you wish to improve the shape of your pony and concentrate on these areas. Wisping can work wonders and give a muscle an extra roundness where beforehand it was lacking, for example between the top of the croup and the tail. Be careful never to wisp a pony over the loins as the kidneys are situated just below this area. Don't bang too hard, just enough to make the muscle flinch. This flinching is what makes the muscle develop.

A pony whose coat shines through pure health and good grooming looks quite different from a pony who has been shampooed. So if you want him to look his best, he must be groomed and cared for in such a way that shampooing is not necessary. Good grooming takes time, especially in the winter when it is necessary to quarter him. This means that his rugs are not taken right off, but turned back only enough to expose the area to be attended. Ponies love to be groomed so give them as much time as you can spare.

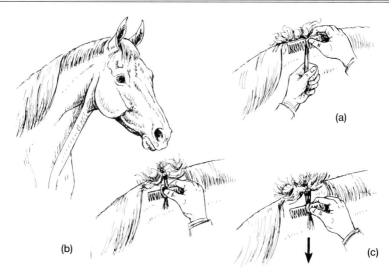

Fig. 3.3 Mane pulling. (a) Grasp a few of the longer hairs and separate by sliding the comb up the mane up to the roots. (b) Twist the hair around the comb. (c) Remove the hairs with a confident pull.

Preparing manes and tails for the ring is something that needs practice. If the pony is a pure-bred indigenous one, he will need to be left as natural as possible if he is to be shown in breed classes. However, for SHP or WHP classes he must have his mane plaited and his tail either pulled or plaited. To pull the mane, take a small amount of hair that is longer than the rest, hold it between the finger and thumb, and push the rest of the hair out of the way with a comb. Twist the piece of hair around the comb and, with a confident pull, draw it out. Keep going until the required length is reached. Be careful not to make the pony sore; just take a little at a time and don't attempt the whole mane in one go.

Explaining how to plait a mane or tail is very difficult, but general guidelines can be given: be confident, do it wet, pull tightly as you go and stitch carefully. The person who sews should always be the person who does the undoing because he or she knows where the stitches are, and is unlikely to cut the mane or tail by mistake. The only way to learn is to practise at home until you do it well, and the best training ground is to go in for lots of 'neat and clean' classes at local shows. You will need to determine how many plaits to put on each pony's neck. As a general guide put more tiny ones on a short neck; if the neck is exceptionally or unpleasantly long, then a smaller number will look better. If you are good at putting elastic bands on your plaits, then use them, because you

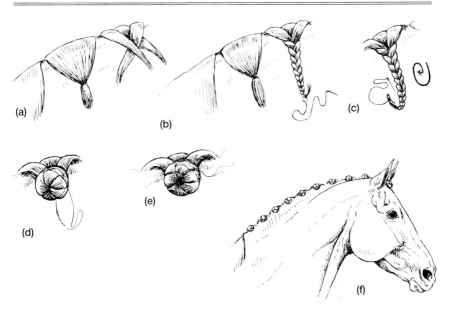

Fig. 3.4 How to plait a mane. (a) Wet the mane and, starting at the top of the mane, use a comb to measure out equal sections. Secure each section with a rubber band. Divide the section to be worked into three strands and start plaiting. (b) Plait tightly down to the end, secure the end with thread, turn the spiky ends under the plait, and stitch in place. (c) Roll up the plait and stitch as you go, so all is secure. (d) Sew the rolled plait in place by passing the needle into the centre and round the sides alternately. Tie tightly. (e) Leave spare end of thread on the plait in case a last-minute repair is needed. Snip off thread ends before entering ring. (f) Work down the mane keeping the plaiting tight and neat.

will not have to use scissors to unplait. Another consideration is the position of the plait. Some ponies look better with the plait right on top of the neck if they have a poor or thin neck. Short thick-set necks look better if the plait is set further down. Taping is usually only used for show-jumpers and dressage horses.

Show grooming techniques

There are several products on the market to help you to improve the turn-out of your pony for the show ring. He should already have a glossy coat produced by good feeding, grooming, and general good health, but if he has been out in the field, he may need a shampoo. For this use a pony shampoo and make sure he does not catch cold by keeping the parts not being washed covered

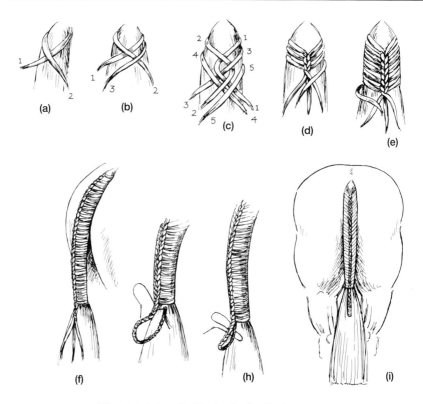

Fig. 3.5 (a) – (i) Method of tail plaiting.

by blankets.

A little Vaseline or baby oil wiped on the lips and upper eyelids will give a polished look. Some people trim off the muzzle whiskers, but you should never cut the eyelashes off.

If the mane has any unruly hairs, in spite of plaiting, these may be controlled by the use of hair spray or egg white. Some people trim away the hair from the poll and from the wither area, but this is not necessary. An extra plait can be put on the wither, which could make the neck look a little longer.

White legs can be a problem. You can use chalk, but this is inclined to shed powder over the hoof – just when the hoof has been oiled. We find tennis-shoe whitener is better, and easier to apply. Add a little water to the applicator and stroke it on. It is particularly good for legs that have awkward white areas.

Adding some Stockholm tar to hoof oil makes the latter a little blacker, which looks very smart when applied. Do not be tempted to use sump oil or hoof paint because these are not good for the horn, and tend to look very unnatural. Make sure the foot is clean, put in studs if required, then oil the hoof including the bulb of the heel. Only use studs when really necessary and remember to remove them immediately after use. If you forget, the pony could injure himself, especially if he lies down in the stable.

Putting squares on your pony's bottom should not be overdone. Practise at home to get the best effect for your pony's shape. You can use a template, but we have never done so, preferring to use a shortened human comb. First draw a line straight down the pony's spine with the comb, then draw one either side of this. From these two new lines you start the patterns, making sure that the squares are the same both sides of the pony. When you have finished, the decoration should look symmetrical when viewed from behind. Put the squares nearer the saddle if the pony has a long back, further away if the back is short.

Now put brush sweeps across the buttock muscles. This is done with a body brush, sometimes wet, and needs some practise. Finally draw the brush from the top of the tail to the right and left

Sefton Tony of Alderbourne – supreme winner in 1981, owner Mr L. Connor. Note the neat markers on his quarters. (Photo: Carol Gilson)

Towy Valley Maurice, owned by Dr and Mrs Micallef, supreme winner in 1987. Note the condition and gloss of his coat. (Photo: Frank Grainger)

to improve the look of the dock area and to cover the ends of the side brush sweeps.

Look at other people's ponies to get ideas, but do be discreet, and do not overdo it.

SHOEING

Choose the best and most reliable farrier in your district, even if he is a little more expensive than the others. You may require a special shoe to help a pony put his foot down correctly, or to avoid over-reaching and brushing, and if your farrier is good he will help and advise you on these matters. You may wish to have a very light pair of shoes in front – this will make a difference to the pony's action – but bear in mind that this type of shoe will not last long on the road.

To have a set of shoes 'removed' means taking them all off, trimming the foot, then replacing the whole set. We don't do this because (a) it is not much cheaper than a new set and (b) it has to be done more frequently so you will get a lot of extra nail-holes in the hoof. We have new sets monthly and find this works very well, but we do quite a lot of road work so the shoes do wear fairly quickly.

If you decide that you want studs in your pony's shoes, be careful to choose the right size. An oversized stud in a small shoe will weaken the metal, so take your farrier's advice. You may have stud holes put in all four shoes, then if the going is particularly slippery your pony will have extra security, but it is more usual to have them in the rear shoes only. Studs in front can be dangerous so do be sure to remove them after use. If a pony lies down in the stable he may damage himself on getting up, particularly his elbows. Remove all studs as soon as you have finished using them, stuff the hole tight with cotton wool and carefully put the studs away.

Try to work on soft ground when studs are fitted as the foot will be put down crookedly on a hard surface.

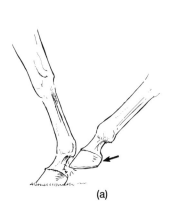
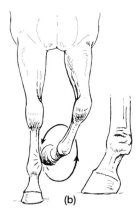

Fig. 3.6 (a) Over-reaching – the hind toe strikes the front heel. Rectify by rolling metal on the toes of hind shoes and by keeping the pony up to the bridle when ridden. (b) Brushing – front foot strikes inside of opposite front leg. Rectify by making inside thickness of offending shoe thinner. The pony will then put down and pick up his foot differently, and thereby improve his action.

WORMING

The amount of worming that has to be carried out depends on the way the pony is kept. If he is out with other ponies all the time, he will need a dose every six weeks; if he is with cattle, perhaps every eight to ten weeks will be enough. If he is kept in the stable, you have much more control over his susceptibility to worms, therefore you will only need to worm him every ten to twelve weeks. If your pony is in poor condition and you suspect worms, then do seek the advice of your vet and possibly have a worm count done, then follow the vet's advice. Otherwise, use a different worm product each time in the hope that what one wormer does not control, the next one will.

Many wormers tell you to use a certain amount of medicine for a given weight of pony. This is not of much use unless you know what your pony weighs, so we have included the table opposite to help you with this problem.

TOOTH RASPING

As ponies' teeth grow all the time, unlike humans, the wearing surfaces will change with the angles of growth. Inspection for uneven wear must be carried out regularly, as rough edges coming into contact with the inside of the cheeks can make a pony very sore. Your vet will be able to rasp the teeth to make them level again.

CLIPPING – WHETHER TO AND WHEN

Whether to clip a pony is usually considered in relation to the winter (novice) season or the early shows, and how we can make him respectable for these. If he has been hunting and hunter trialing and has already been clipped he may just need tidying while the summer coat comes through, giving extra attention to whiskers, mane, tail and fetlocks. If he is not already clipped, you may bring him in in early February, rug him up well and encourage his winter coat to come away early. This gives a good result. Bear in mind when clipping that a winter coat usually finishes growing by the end of December, and the summer coat can begin to grow as

Weight		Type	Size	Dosage
kg	lb			
up to 300	660	Donkeys, Shetlands, Welsh Mountain, etc.	up to 12.2 hh	
300-450	990	Dartmoor, New Forest, Welsh, etc.	12.2 hh – 14.2 hh	As prescribed on the packet
450-600	1320	TB, Arabs, Hacks, light hunters	14.2 hh – 16 hh	
600-700	1540	Mid-heavy hunters	16 hh and over	
750 and over	1650 and over	Heavy draught horses	16 hh	

NB: These weights given are for adult horses and ponies, but mares in foal and foals must be wormed according to the vet's advice.

early as January. So any clipping done after this can actually cut into the new summer coat. A late clip may take until May or even June on an indigenous pony to grow out properly and this shows, particularly if a saddle patch or other shapes are left on. Mountain and moorland ponies can be a problem, though. Some seem to have a summer coat only for June and July and spend the rest of the year growing a new one or casting off the old one.

WINTERING

It is both unkind and unwise to put an unclipped pony out on a cold evening when he is hot and sweaty. You are also asking for trouble if you take an unfit, unclipped pony hunting during the Christmas holidays, and then chuck him out into the field, even if he has a rug on.

If you are working your pony in the winter he will need to be either partially or totally clipped otherwise he will become very hot, sweaty and extremely uncomfortable and may seriously lose condition. When he sweats, he will lose a lot of moisture, and his blood will be working overtime trying to keep him cool. All this uses up his resources, therefore he will lose weight and easily become breathless.

When he is not working, a clipped pony will need the protection of a rug, both in and out of the stable. The amount of clothing he needs depends on the temperature, so he may need blankets underneath his rug if it is very cold. When a pony is in work in the winter, he should be having a fair amount of food, and there is no point in allowing this expensive commodity to evaporate into thin air – so keep him warm.

A partial clip will still be evident if he is shown in the spring. Provided this is done neatly we would not penalise him since we approve of ponies being used, but other owners and judges have different opinions.

If your pony is not working in the winter there is no need to clip him, and certainly in the first half of the winter he is better off without rugs. This will encourage his coat to grow. A healthy well-fed pony with a good natural coat will withstand any amount of cold, but days of continuous rain with blustering winds could cause a problem. Look out for shivering in these conditions. Ponies are not very sensible about using a field shelter; sometimes a bossy pony will monopolise a shelter and keep the others out. Bring shivering ponies in and rub them down to dry them. Put them out again when the weather dries up. We thatch our ponies with a thick layer of clean straw under a rug whilst they dry off.

Do not use a New Zealand rug on an unclipped pony out of sentiment; it is probably unnecessary if you proceed as above; nor does it relieve you of the responsibility of keeping an eye on the animal. Remember: any form of rugging up flattens the coat and, if this happens, the insulating layer of air is lost.

You will need two New Zealand rugs for each pony. New Zealands can get saturated in prolonged wet conditions, and, unless in good condition, can leak. You will therefore need to fetch your pony in occasionally to change his rug and dry the wet one. In the spring the rugs can wear away the new coat on the points of the shoulders, which looks ugly in the show ring, but this should not happen if the rugs fit properly.

If you are out-wintering a pony it is not a good idea to groom him more than is necessary because grooming removes the protective grease and mud from the coat, and he will lose his natural weather protection. However, you must check over his legs and feet occasionally.

Another wintering alternative, applicable to a 'pensioner' or lighter-coated pony who has not been clipped, is to have him out during the day and in at night. He will need a rug in the stable because he cannot move about to keep warm as he would outside, and may get chilly from draughts. Having cleaned him to put on his night rug, and flattened his coat with the rug, he will have lost some natural protection and will need a New Zealand rug outside too.

It is very difficult to keep a pony in work during the winter, even minimally, unless you have a loose box. Sometimes people without stabling facilities put out a pony with a full or partial coat in a New Zealand rug right at the start of the winter for their own convenience, i.e. so that he is cleaner and the work in preparing him for the occasional ride is reduced. But here you have to be very careful not to sweat him up and it is not a recommended method of management. Without proper facilities and/or time, you would be wiser to simply maintain your pony over the winter, and prepare him for the show ring in the spring, foregoing the early shows.

The best way to work a pony in the winter is to have him fully clipped and stabled. It entails a lot of work for he will need exercising every day (except perhaps the day after hunting), so the decision to opt for this form of management should not be undertaken lightly. However, you do have full control of his conditions. You can occasionally put him out for a few hours, well wrapped up, to relieve boredom.

If you do not wish to work him seriously over the winter but are keen for him to be ready for the spring shows, then an alternative is to keep him out after the Peterborough championships to grow a coat. This is easier with hunter ponies as opposed to show ponies as they do not have to be kept in summer coat until Wembley in October, when it is quite cold at night, and too much of a shock to the system to go out in the field.

Bring your pony in after Christmas. If he is rugged up he will lose his winter coat early. He will need grooming and regular light exercise to reduce boredom. The work can increase as the showing season approaches and you can have him looking really well to give him a good start to the season.

To look good in the spring, whatever method of winter management you select, he must be properly fed in the winter. His feeding will need to be adjusted depending on whether you are just maintaining him or working him. Condition lost in the winter is not quickly recovered in the spring. Just because you are not using him, do not forget that his feet will need regular attention and that your worming programme must be continued.

During the winter, owing to the weather, it is very easy to forget to go round your fields to check the fences and water troughs. However, this must be done just as often as in the summer.

Managing ponies throughout the winter will not be kind to your hands and you may develop chaps. To avoid this try the following: wear rubber gloves under another pair of gloves, preferably woolly ones. Put on handcream first. The rubber gloves will keep your hands dry, but moist and warm, however wet the work; the woolly ones will keep you warm and protect the rubber ones from being damaged. Sugar-beet is notorious for chapping the skin, so avoid contact with the bare hands.

INSURANCE

Insurance is a business deal and is governed primarily by the terms of the policy, so it is important that you enter into the contract knowing exactly how you stand, because insurance never covers every eventuality. If you do not fully understand the conditions, ask the broker or agent to explain them to you.

For preference, deal with a broker who knows about ponies. A good broker regards himself as buying insurance on your behalf from an underwriter, looking after your interests first, rather than regarding himself as selling you a policy. Do remember, however, that he makes his living out of the commission he receives on the policy, so his interests are not entirely parallel with yours. Read the small print.

If you wish, you could cut out the broker and go straight to an insurance company, but you will probably be offered only one policy and will not get the advice of a broker, who could shop around to find a policy suitable for your requirements and the best cover for your premium.

The annual premium will depend upon three factors: the insured value of the animal, the risks you wish to cover, and the use to which you wish to put the animal. For example, if you wish to insure a working hunter pony to include Pony Club events, hunting and show-jumping, then you will probably have to pay in the region of six to eight per cent of the insured value per annum. This should cover you for accidental fatal injuries, fatal illnesses, humane destruction, theft, straying and lightning strikes, with partial cover for loss of use in case the animal has to be prematurely retired. Insurance does not extend to paying veterinary fees unless the policy specifically says so, and you will find that you will probably not receive compensation for blemishes.

Always remember that as your pony increases in value through his successes it is wise to update the sum for which he is insured.

In the event or possibility of making a claim it is very important that you keep the insurance company fully informed, as this is always a condition of the policy. For example, if your pony seems to be ill or has had an accident you must let the insurance company know immediately. Your vet will advise you about this, and it may not be necessary for a slight indisposition. As an example, if you decide to have a bony enlargement removed from one of your pony's legs and he fails to regain consciousness after an anaesthetic, you would not be able to claim on your insurance unless you had the insurance company's prior permission to go ahead with the operation. The principle seems to be that once the animal is insured, the insurers have a financial interest in the pony and a legal right to know what is happening.

It is advisable to insure your tack, and for a little extra money this can usually be added to a policy. Keep an up-to-date list of all the tack that you own, keep it well repaired and try to have some way of identifying it in case it is stolen. Ask your broker also about third-party insurance, so that you do not have the worry of claims against you on behalf of your pony's actions and misdemeanours. It is possible that this is covered by your household policy. It is very important to have this cover for although liability claims of this nature are relatively rare, they are usually for ruinous amounts.

Policies are normally issued on a renewable basis, but insurers do not usually have any obligation to renew on the same terms as previously. You may find that if you report trouble during the currency of a policy, they may try to impose extra conditions on renewal, e.g. 'liability for right foreleg excluded'.

Remember, everything is negotiable and in cases of doubt insurers will sometimes offer an ex-gratia payment without prejudice for the sake of good will.

CHAPTER 4

Hunter Pony Type, Action and Conformation

HUNTER PONY TYPE

It has been stated many times that good conformation is the same irrespective of breed or type; speakers then go on to explain good points of conformation of a horse or pony. This is both remarkable and confusing, for quite clearly a good Shire horse and a good Thoroughbred are very different although they may both be winners in their own sphere. Just what is the difference between the Thoroughbred and the Shire? It is a matter of type: they are diametrically different types. We like to define type as emphasis of conformation depending on the work to which the animal is to be put. It is a lot to do with the relative positions of the points of the horse.

So, what of the hunter pony's work? First and foremost, by definition, he must be capable of taking a child hunting – this militates against any weakness in conformation which would prevent this – and he must do it comfortably and safely for his young rider. Secondly, he will be required to tackle WHP classes, so he must be able to jump a reasonable course of fences, although this does not have such a bearing on conformation as the first consideration, for it is well known that show-jumpers come in all shapes and sizes. Jumping ability stems more from the pony's mind, his training and the mind of the rider. However, unsuitable conformation will predispose to premature wear and failure, especially continual work on hard ground.

We have put these two requirements first because 50 per cent of the marks in a WHP class are allotted to the jumping, plus 10 per cent for manners whilst jumping, with a further 10 per cent for manners whilst performing a show, and 30 per cent for conformation, type and freedom of action. So 70 per cent of the marks are allotted to performance in the broadest sense of the word, against only 30 per cent for conformation. Although working hunter pony competitions are rightly described as performance classes, we believe that, if our standard of judging conformation is correct, good conformation plays an important part in the ability to stay sound to do this work; also for the other work which we believe ponies need to keep them interested and alert. Furthermore, as explained later, we believe it affects the 20 per cent for manners too, for a young pony of the 'right shape' will find it easier to do his work without discomfort.

Having defined the work of a hunter pony we must now ask what particular attributes this type of pony requires and how they differ from other ponies, particularly show ponies. However, let it first be said that all sorts of ponies compete in WHP classes successfully and just because they are not what someone else feels to be the ideal they should not be discouraged from competing. The marking is such that 70 per cent of the points are awarded for performance, and this is as it should be. So if a pony goes well, whatever its type, it stands a good chance of winning, and good luck to it.

In the show hunter pony classes there is no jumping phase so the emphasis is more on the conformation and action, but we are talking about the same animal. We cannot subscribe to any idea of the SHP and WHP being in any way different from each other except for wear and blemish. In judging a show hunter pony we must be looking for the ideal child's hunter and any suggestion that it can have a lower action or less bone than a WHP, or any other difference, is complete nonsense in our view.

All of us, unless we have absolutely no knowledge of the subject or unless we are stable blind, know that our ponies may not quite be the ideal type for the job, and if we waited to find the perfect horse we would wait for ever. This is not to say, however, that we shouldn't have in our mind's eye a picture of the ideal hunter pony type for which we should strive and for which our judges should look. What should this be?

This is a controversial question, but the late Count Orsich made some interesting remarks in *Horse and Hound* and we make no apology for quoting this authority.

> When someone asks me what I look for in a show horse my answer is: type, then conformation, action, ride, age, and

temperament... In my opinion there are five different types of show horse – hunter, hack, cob, pony, and Arab. Type is very important as nothing is worse than to put a square peg in a round hole. An example is showing an overgrown show pony or a good hunter in a show hack class, a hack in a small (15.2 hh) hunter class, or a small hack in the working hunter pony class under 15 hh. With good judges this is never successful, hence such terms as too ponified, too hacky, or not hunter type; and put down the line however well the animal went. It is not bad luck but good judging.

Who are we to disagree? We believe that, foremost, judges should be looking for a definite hunter type, and that their priorities should be:

Type

then

Conformation

then

Action

then

Temperament

Having said that, we would probably put temperament near the top of the list in the cradle and nursery stakes classes, although any really bad faults of conformation, action, or temperament would disqualify a pony from high marks.

Nevertheless, we would rather see a pony of the right type with minor conformation or action faults with top marks than a pony of the wrong type with near perfect conformation. In other words, as judges we have no right to put up the animal we like best if it does not fit the class description.

You will notice that we have missed 'age' out of the above list for we feel that this is of secondary importance as long as the pony is four years or older, has the necessary experience, is sound and in good condition and is not showing too much sign of wear. Age should not be of prime importance, although, again, wear might be more excusable in the cradle or nursery stakes or the 12 hh SHP class where safety and confidence-giving are the first considerations.

Broadgates Spangle, an excellent small hunter type – good enough for height estimation to be very difficult. (Photo: J. Thorne)

We have also missed out 'ride' in the above list, because the judge is not allowed to ride hunter ponies so he has to judge this aspect at arm's length. Whether or not the child gets a good ride is nevertheless very important and cannot be ignored, and a knowledgeable judge will have a pretty good idea of what sort of ride a pony is giving. This may affect manners, conformation and action marks.

We have not mentioned 'presence' as there are no marks for this quality in WHP classes, but what show animal is not better for this attribute? This is the quality which says 'Look at me' and 'I am', which must be a lot to do with what showing is all about.

When a new class is introduced it tends to become a 'dustbin' for all the ponies which fit the size specification but which have not made it in other directions. This tended to be the case with WHPs in the early 1970s: the owners of show ponies who were not doing too well responded by teaching them to jump and to enter WHP classes. Breeders of pony stock which had overgrown, for instance were over 14.2 hh, but were not suitable for small hack classes, saw the WHP class as an outlet for their produce. Owners and breeders of mountain and moorland ponies also saw the possibilities, and anyone who had a reasonably good-looking show-jumper (and they come in all shapes and sizes), which would not jump the high BSJA courses, considered the smaller WHP fences offered them an opportunity. Any of them performing well, justifiably won and will continue to do so, but it did give the classes an unfortunate reputation as being for ponies that had not succeeded in other circles. As a result, in the eyes of many misguided people, hunter ponies are still regarded as second-class citizens in the pony world.

A sad example of this faulty attitude was exposed in the *Horse and Hound* report on the 1983 spring championship show when the reporter wrote of the hunter type pony classes: 'they provide a second class and a chance for the child with a below top-class pony with a chance to shine'.

In the horse world people do not make these sort of comparisons: do you ever hear of a hunter being described as an inferior animal to the hack? They are different, and so it is with ponies.

In attempting to define the hunter type we would like to refer to the specifications of the Hunter Pony Stud Book Register:

> Correct conformation for riding and endurance.
> Substance without coarseness.
> Quality without fineness.
> Straightness and freedom of action at all paces.
> Natural balance.
> Jumping ability and boldness.
> Steady temperament suitable for a child.
> Colour immaterial.

We are taught to look for a pony with a small fine head, indeed the classical description of a good horse goes something like this: 'Having a head like a lady's maid and the behind of a cook'. That this ideal is not frequently achieved perhaps gives us a clue as to why good show hunters generally do not possess the fine heads of hacks and show ponies.

Think about humans. Those with light bone structure are likely to be light all through – people taking a small size in shoes are most likely also to use small gloves and hats. Conversely those with larger feet and hands are likely to take a large size in hats irrespective of their height; if they do not, then they would be out of proportion. Our observation is that the same is largely true of equines; in a hack or show pony class you need a small, pretty head. Those with fine heads will probably be finely boned throughout and have smaller joints and dainty feet. These make the hacks and show ponies of this world, and their lightness of structure is consistent with their elegance and lightness of movement.

This brings us to our point that type depends on the purpose for which the horse or pony is required: a hunter is required to stand up to a lot more hard work, probably on rougher going than the hack, so the type specification for a hunter and a hunter pony type embrace the qualities desirable for their work.

A good hunter judge will be looking for a good back end, strong quarters and hocks with forelimbs to match, and these must be his main considerations. More about these attributes later, but it follows that this well-boned hunter type, like the person with the large shoes, will have a somewhat larger head than the show pony, but this does not preclude 'quality' nor imply a common head. There is a tendency to look business-like rather than pretty, with an overall well-proportioned athletic appearance and a square stance on four good limbs with plenty of bone. A pony that stands thus, will be sure-footed. This is in contrast to a pony which is narrow, and shows a lot of daylight; this type of pony will be more likely to fall because his feet are nearer together and his centre of gravity is high.

When we discuss type we must not forget that the different sizes of pony are very slightly different types within their own size groups, i.e.:

Cradle Stakes – a small pony with substance, a definite place for the saddle, but overall a very safe pony for a small child to ride.

Nursery Stakes – a bigger version of the cradle stakes pony but with a little more scope, probably not over 12.2 hh, again very safe and trustworthy, and able to take a child over fences without pulling. These two small ponies must always be of genuine nature, honest, and with no spiteful tendencies. Manners and performance will take precedence over conformation.

13 hh – this pony along with the 14 hh version should be like a real miniature middleweight and epitomises the true hunter pony type. Both will be ridden by children who are accomplished so can be

However good their conformation, cradle stakes ponies must have excellent, steady temperaments. (Photo: J. Thorne)

expected to be more able to cope with more talent.

15 hh – this pony will also be a miniature middleweight type, and he will be less of a pony; this is because he is bound to have some horse breeding in him, along with blood from the bigger indigenous breeds.

The four smaller groups, that is, the cradle stakes, the nursery stakes, the 13 hh and 14 hh ponies, will have a great deal more indigenous pony blood in their veins, with perhaps a little riding pony, a little Arab, or a little Thoroughbred.

Slightly different patterns of breeding will be used for the different sizes, but it is all a case of emphasis. It may take several generations to arrive at the type of animal required.

ACTION

You may wonder why it is so important for a pony to have straight action when viewed from the front or behind. There are many reasons.

Firstly, a straight mover is demonstrating that his legs are put together correctly, i.e. all the joints from the hoof through the fetlock, knee, elbow and the point of the shoulder in front, and through the fetlock, hock, stifle, and hip joint behind, are above each other in the same vertical plane. If they are not, then as the pony moves he will put undue pressure on one side of the articulating surfaces of his joints instead of evenly. The pressure will therefore be concentrated and wear will be more rapid.

Secondly, a straight mover will not kick himself, whereas a pony whose legs are not properly aligned will swing them about at unnatural angles, will strike his other legs, and put his feet down unevenly on the ground. In turn, this will make him wear his feet unevenly, his shoes will show signs of wear in odd places, and his feet will have to be shod more often, probably with corrective shoes. The corrective shoes themselves will apply uneven pressure to the joints.

Thirdly, a straight mover is less likely to trip himself up. A bad mover may damage himself very badly and may actually fall over, particularly on corners. This is an obvious danger to his jockey.

Fourthly, any deviation from the straight is a waste of effort by the pony as it does not contribute to his forward progression over the ground. A bad mover will not last as long and will be prone to unsoundness.

Straightness of action

To assess the straightness of the action of a pony you will need to see him both walked and trotted towards you and away from you in straight lines on a hard surface, which must be level.

First, the front view. Observe him standing. Are his forelegs straight, and upright? Do his toes point straight in front? Is there room for his elbows to move without fouling his ribs? When he moves towards you, are his feet put down squarely, or outside first? When he picks his feet up do they trail straight behind, dish outwards or turn inwards? Dishing is ugly, and turning inwards is dangerous due to the possibility of tripping and self injury. Are the feet put down the same distance apart as his knees or are they put one in front of the other (plaiting)? When the lower leg is swung back from the knee does it go straight back and when pulled forwards and straightened, is it at all times in the same plane? Or does it swing towards the other leg?

Is the action from the point of the shoulder straight or do the forelegs move with a paddling action right from the top? If you want to see his action at the front at its worst, make him trot towards you downhill. If the pony is very fat this can spoil his action, especially at the front because the elbow cannot move straight backwards causing the lower leg to swing out.

Now the back view. Are his feet the same distance apart as the hocks? When he moves do his feet go straight forwards to track up, or wide, i.e. put down outside his forelegs? Do his feet point outwards as the fetlocks flex when the weight is taken? Do his hocks move straight or do they sway outwards as they take the load? – a definite weakness. Does he move close behind so that there is a danger of one foot knocking the other leg? – a fault that far too many horses suffer from.

Movement

Another aspect of action is the way the pony actually moves his legs and the pattern they describe when viewed from the side. This is affected by the length of the long bones of the legs, e.g. if the leg has a long forearm and a longer cannon bone then we can expect the action to be higher, i.e. more knee action, or a round action.

A low mover can have considerable advantages. As a sprinter, he will not waste his energy lifting his feet higher above the ground than is absolutely necessary. This is all right for racehorses, for race tracks are smooth. For the park hack, a low action gives a more comfortable ride, especially side-saddle. Again he will be on smooth going, so that is fine. No one can deny the attractive appearance of a Thoroughbred or show pony moving effortlessly and gracefully round the ring with a low action, but there is an element of fashion in this; a hundred years ago horse dealers used to go to great lengths to make their stock pick up their feet when trotted out for a customer.

However, hunters are a different matter, the going will not always be smooth, so they must pick their feet up rather more. Some knee action is necessary. We are not recommending a high knee action like a Hackney or Welsh cob – moderation is called for. The movement should be neither too high nor too low. A pony with a daisy-cutting action is the wrong type and should not win a hunter class.

By studying the diagrams we can see just one example of how the action of the horse's legs is far more complicated than our own. We only have one bone between our knee and our hip joint, whereas apart from any movement of the shoulder blade, which can be observed from the ground, when the points of the left and right shoulder move alternately forward as each foreleg reaches forward, the horse's action hinges from the point of the shoulder, and there are two bones (the humerus and the radius) between that joint and the knee and an extra joint at the elbow. The illustrations show how the horse makes use of his extra facilities to increase the effective length of his leg and cover the ground. If a pony is observed walking, the important movement of the humerus can be clearly seen. A pony which does this energetically is known as a good walker because it moves 'from the shoulder'. A good walker is generally a good trotter, and a good galloper. It should be noted that a good mover needs time to show off his action; if you move him with a fast walk or trot you will limit his action. So keep the paces slow but active.

Many horses and ponies do not swing their humerus as they

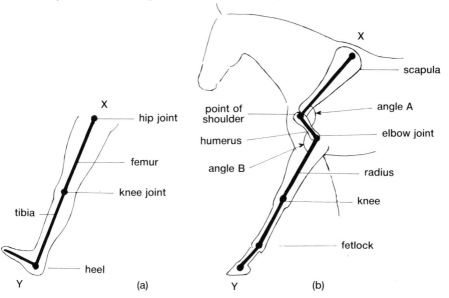

Fig. 4.1 (a) Human leg at the walk. Notice how the maximum distance between the hip joint (X) and the heel (Y) is fixed by the total length of the femur and tibia. Compare this with the horse's foreleg at the walk, shown in (b). Notice how in the horse the humerus hinges at the point of the shoulder and elbow, allowing both angles A and B increase, actually extending the total length of the leg from the withers (X) to the heel (Y) in order to cover more ground with the stride.

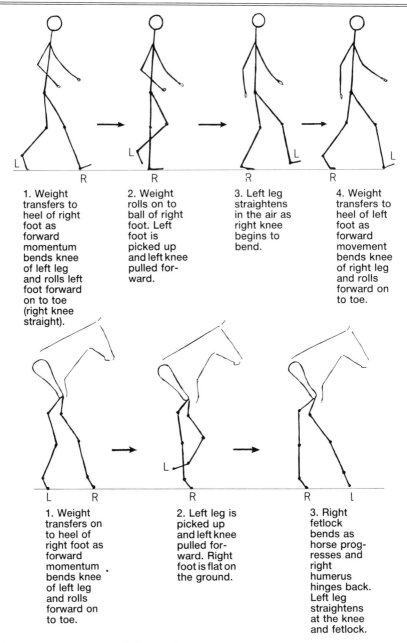

1. Weight transfers to heel of right foot as forward momentum bends knee of left leg and rolls left foot forward on to toe (right knee straight).

2. Weight rolls on to ball of right foot. Left foot is picked up and left knee pulled forward.

3. Left leg straightens in the air as right knee begins to bend.

4. Weight transfers to heel of left foot as forward movement bends knee of right leg and rolls forward on to toe.

1. Weight transfers on to heel of right foot as forward momentum bends knee of left leg and rolls forward on to toe.

2. Left leg is picked up and left knee pulled forward. Right foot is flat on the ground.

3. Right fetlock bends as horse progresses and right humerus hinges back. Left leg straightens at the knee and fetlock.

Fig. 4.2 Comparison of the walking action of human and horse (forelegs only). The construction of the horse's foreleg enables him to extend the length of his stride, whereas a human does not have this ability. NB: The same principles apply to the hind leg of the horse, but are not quite as clear to observe in operation.

should, in this case the action hinges not from the point of the shoulder but more from the elbow. This is known as 'moving from the elbow' and is an inferior action for the pony does not use himself to advantage – he needs to take more paces to cover a given distance than one which moves from the shoulder. Clearly there is much more to the study of locomotion, but this illustration shows just how well endowed the horse is for moving across country fast, and emphasises the importance of free and correct action. The action of a hunter is very important, not just for aesthetic reasons, but for the very practical considerations which we have demonstrated.

Mood also has an effect on a pony's movement. When we feel light-hearted we often have a spring in our step. So it is with your pony. You may have noticed how he moves around his paddock when he is excited. He will move in a more extravagant way than usual, and he will 'show off'. If your pony has presence in the show ring, he will probably move more extravagantly than he usually does, and this will make him an extra pleasure to watch.

ASSESSING CONFORMATION

Conformation has to do with the bones, the skeleton, the soft tissues, the muscles, the tendons, and the ligaments. Early feeding, water and other environmental factors complete the picture. But what do you look for when assessing a pony, and where do you start?

We like to stand back and look at the animal as a whole. Apart from the question of type in relation to the job the pony has to do, we ask ourselves whether the pony in its entirety pleases us. Does the back look as if it belongs to the front? Does the top belong to the bottom, or does it look like an 'a.s.p.' (all spare parts!)? Taking the first question, a good front impresses us all, but in a hunter the back end, the engine, must look strong; a hunter which tails off from the front is not right.

We look for a good top, not too long, not too short; but a pony with plenty of top must have the legs to carry it. A flashy pony with inadequate legs is not a hunter type. A pony can carry a lot of condition, and this will vary from time to time depending on his feeding, his work and his age; but you cannot hope that a

Just So, owned by Mrs Heal. Note the good conformation and imagine the comfortable ride.

fully grown pony will produce more bone – that depends on his genes, the feeding of his dam and his own feeding as a youngster. Substance is not fatness, nor is it muscle – it is the framework as well.

Having walked round the pony at some distance and formed an initial impression, you will have already made an assessment of his shoulder, head, neck, chest, abdomen, quarters. Is there too much daylight under him, i.e. is he 'on the leg'? Are his legs too long in relation to the depth of his body? Now look at his legs in some detail; a hunter pony will do a lot of work in his life, so he must have good legs.

POINTS OF CONFORMATION

Feet

Are they of the right size, in proportion to the rest of the animal? Small feet are too dainty in a hunter. Small feet go with small joints, and anyway are more likely to sink into soft going. If too large they appear common and clumsy and frequently go with common legs. Feet should be neither too flat, flared out, nor too upright (boxy). A flat foot can be the cause of much lameness. The sole, being near the ground, can bruise easily on stones. Shoeing can also give trouble – due to the angle of the foot the point of the nail which the farrier 'clenches' is too near the edge and pulls away. This damages the edge of the hoof and makes reshoeing difficult. Consequently if the shoes are left off, the edges can break away exacerbating the problem.

On the other hand, boxy feet create their own set of problems, the main one being that the frog does not come into contact with the ground. The proper functioning of the frog is very important: it is intended to press on the ground to provide a cushioning effect, and its action is important to the health of the foot. Boxy feet are usually associated with upright pasterns, and the consequent lack of shock absorption can result in serious diseases, particularly navicular, pedalostitis, side bone and ringbone.

Hard feet are a great advantage since they do not break away so easily, it is certainly our experience that dark feet are harder than white feet, although not everybody would agree on this point.

Pasterns

The length of the long pastern bone is a most important aspect. As with the feet, extremes are to be avoided. Short pasterns tend to be upright with consequent loss of springiness. They cause the full shockload of footfall to be borne by the articulating joints on the bony parts and the cartilage between them, and this is especially serious on hard going. Long pasterns tend to slope more and yield to slope further on the impact of the foot. This action relieves the load on the joints but transmits it to the soft connective tissue, namely the flexor tendons. In extreme conditions this can lead to tendon strain. Racehorses tend to have long pasterns, which is no doubt a factor in their ability to sprint, but they 'go' in the leg which usually means sprained flexor tendons in the forelegs. By the way, it is normal for hind pasterns to be just slightly more upright than those in the fore.

Fetlocks

These, like the feet, should be in proportion to the remainder of the animal. Undersized fetlocks will be unable to withstand the pressures on the bearing surfaces of these joints and are therefore

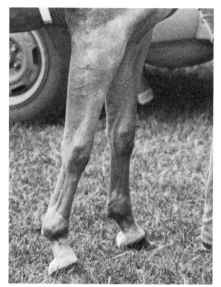

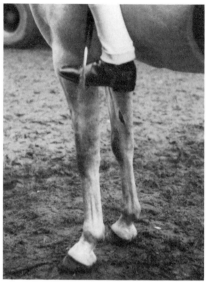

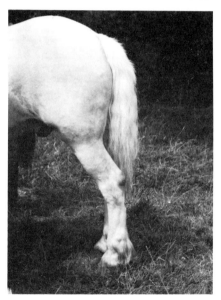

(ABOVE LEFT) *Quality legs – long fore-arm, short cannon, well-developed trapezium bone, but fetlocks look 'appley'. More of a show pony type – likely to be a low mover; insufficient bone for the hunter type. The fetlock joints are too small to take the continual pounding of the hunter.*
(ABOVE RIGHT) *Weak legs. Inadequate bone below the knee, round knees and lack of prominent trapezium bone behind the knees can be seen, even from this angle.*
(LEFT) *Common legs – short, upright pasterns, gummy legs and puffy joints. Hair in the heel is not a fault in itself, but is frequently associated with this type of pastern.* (Photo: *J. Thorne*)

to be avoided. Fetlock wear is manifested as windgalls, i.e. soft lumpy enlargements above the joint, more common in the summer when the ground is hard, especially in the hind. They are more excusable in older ponies that have done a lot of work, but very undesirable in young ponies, and, of course, in show hunter ponies, which are better unblemished.

Cannon bones

Cannon bones are usually preferred short. This is to do with action and strength. In quality legs, it will be possible to see the suspensory ligaments and flexor tendons, whereas in the more common leg this is not the case.

Knees

Knees are very complicated structures. Like fetlocks they contain bearing surfaces and therefore must be up to size. Furthermore the trapezium bone, which sticks out at the back, is important to observe. The flexor tendons pass over the back of it and it must be large enough to give leverage to the tendon to minimise stress. The width of the knee from the front view is also important to minimise uneven joint pressure and strain of ligaments induced by, for example, sideways sloping ground, treading on a stone on one side of a foot, or just cornering at speed. Small knees are thus highly undesirable. A quality knee is flat across the front and looks angular in outline when viewed from the front. It should never be a round shape.

Hocks

The hock is another complicated joint with articulating surfaces, and the 'os calcis' at the point of the hock must be amply proportioned to transmit the burden of the powerful muscles above and convert to a propelling force. The whole hock must be large enough in proportion to the remainder of the pony for reasons of minimising the joint load and the forces of the tendons. Wear or weakness of the hock is revealed by soft swellings known as bog spavins on the front surface; or thoroughpins, lumps above the point of the hock in the hollow just in front of the flexor tendon. The latter can be pushed from side to side. Hard lesions, e.g. bone spavins, usually on the inside surface near the bottom of the hock, or curbs on the outside surfaces, can be serious and must be suspect.

Upper leg

Apart from perhaps good quarters and bone, the greatest difference between the hack and the hunter, or between the show pony and hunter pony, is in the conformation of the upper legs, i.e. the forearm and second thigh or gaskin. What we look for here is a strong natural development of muscle which is essential to enable him to lift his feet up in rough country and heavy going, and this should be the case in both fore and hind legs.

The set of the hind leg

The easiest way to judge this is to have the pony stand with his hind cannon bones vertical, then stand to one side, level with his hind leg. Now drop an imaginary plumb line down from the point of the buttocks. The hocks should not lie behind this line. If they do, they are known as sickle hocks; they are too bent and definitely not preferred by judges in show classes.

However, we have had several ponies with this fault pass through our hands, and none of them has given us any problems with their hocks, in spite of doing a lot of work over many years. On the contrary, it is the ones with upright hind legs, whose hocks have a tendency to be underneath, which have had problems. Other opinions have tended to confirm this observation: one, a respected vet, prefers hunters to be not too upright behind; and a very experienced dressage rider says that horses with very straight legs are less able to do advanced movements.

Another expert opinion states that when a pony is required to turn abruptly (e.g. in polo or gymkhanas) a slightly sickle hock is acceptable especially if well let down. However, racing people prefer the straighter leg and show judges definitely do, so we cannot go against the tide. Like so many points of conformation a compromise is the order of the day; if the point of the hock is exactly on a line drawn down from the back of the quarters then you will not be far wrong.

When assessing the hind legs, take a view from behind; if necessary ask someone to pull the tail to one side, and make the pony stand square. The legs should not be too close together so that the overall effect is one of narrowness. The hocks should be over the feet so that the weight is carried symmetrically on the joints. If the hocks are closer together than the feet, the animal is cow hocked. This is a weakness. If the feet are closer together than the hocks, the pony is potentially unsound.

The feet should point straight in front, not to one side or inwards, i.e. neither splay-footed nor pin-toed. The overall view

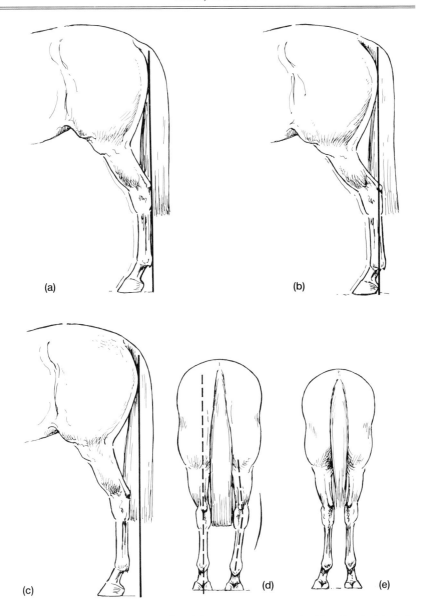

Fig. 4.3 Correct and incorrect hind legs. (a) Correct. (b) Too far behind the vertical. (c) Too straight. (d) Weak hocks. (e) Too narrow and feet turned out.

from the rear should be one of great muscle development, ample quarters and gaskins; the horse should not be 'split' high up between the legs. The joints should be placed one above the next in the same vertical plane so that the wear is even.

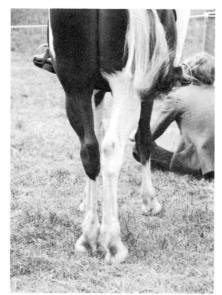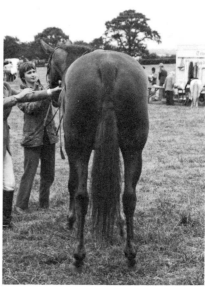

(LEFT) *Close behind. Both hind feet turn outwards.* (RIGHT) *An impressive back end.* (Photos: *J. Thorne*)

The front

The profile of the front end of the pony is the combined effect of many points of conformation, notably: the shoulder blade – its length and angle; the length of the humerus; the depth of the thorax (chest); the position of the wither; the length of the neck; and the head; and all these points of conformation are related.

Consider first the angle of the shoulder blade. We like this well laid back, i.e. much nearer the horizontal than the vertical (see Fig. 4.4b). This has the effect of shortening the neck. In Fig. 4.4a the shoulder is upright but notice how the top of the neck looks longer. Of course it depends where you measure the neck when you eye up a horse – top or bottom? We prefer to think in terms of length of rein not length of neck.

Mrs I. Yeomans, that fount of conformation knowledge, has commented several times that it is most alarming to ride over country on a horse with a long neck set on an upright shoulder; you feel as if you are going over the top, especially downhill. A long neck set on an upright shoulder is frequently associated with a ewe neck, one which looks fitted on upside-down.

If you look just at the head and neck of Fig. 4.4a, and ignore the shoulder, you could say that it would make an attractive

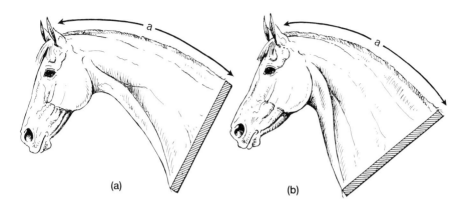

Fig. 4.4 The angle of the shoulder blade has the effect of visually shortening or lengthening the neck. The length of neck (dimension 'a') is the same in both drawings, but the horse with the more upright shoulder blade appears to have the longer neck.

show horse. There is plenty of room and freedom for the windpipe to operate without constriction, and it is elegant. However, it is likely to be heavy on its forehand, a bit bumpy to ride, and, though flexible, will tend to be willowy; its direction and speed would also be difficult to control. This sort of horse is frequently seen going along with its head hanging down, leaning on the bit, both itself and its rider looking miserable. On the other hand, Fig. 4.4b, the other extreme, might receive good marks in a Welsh cob class, but would hardly be right for a show hack class, a hunter or on the racecourse, nor indeed in a smaller version for a child's pony. Why? The shoulder is well laid back?

Fig. 4.5 Ideal angle of shoulder blade for a hunter pony.

Well, a horse like this is more likely to have difficulty in breathing on an extended gallop; and we would want convincing that it did not take hold with a small child before we bought it.

What, then, is the ideal angle of the shoulder blade for a hunter pony? It has to be something between Fig. 4.4a and Fig. 4.4b, like Fig. 4.5, for instance. The illustrations attempt to show that conformation, like design, is a compromise and a matter of opinion, and a single point of conformation cannot be considered in isolation.

Head and neck

A pony uses its head, as a gymnast does, to balance himself. He must move his head from side to side, up and down, and shorten and lengthen his neck as the situation demands. A pony with a shorter neck needs a heavier head to balance himself. If the neck is too short, however, there is likely to be a kink in the windpipe, which limits the pony's air intake, thus his performance, and makes him very uncomfortable. For this reason we like to see a small radius rather than a sharp angle underneath where the neck joins the head (see Fig. 4.6) and this implies a certain length of neck. Now for a pony to be well boned, which we desire, its skull will tend to be larger than a lightly boned pony (remember that people who wear big shoes usually need big hats). It would be inappropriate for a pony with a slightly larger head to have a neck as long as a lighter-boned animal. That type soon tires and tries to lean on your hands.

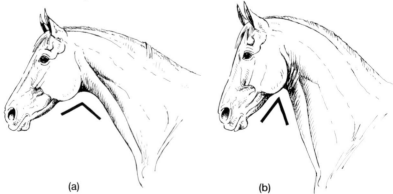

(a)   (b)

Fig. 4.6 (a) The angle between the head and neck allows plenty of room for the windpipe and therefore facilitates breathing. (b) The neck meets the head at too sharp an angle, constricting the breathing.

Forelegs

These do a lot of work: they take the load, propelling the pony forward with the suspension phase of the gallop and landing from a jump. In both cases the knee joint is virtually straight so the shock is absorbed firstly by the flexing of the fetlock joint angle, then by the shoulder, the angle between the shoulder blade and the humerus. The forces are transmitted via the tendons to the muscles which are attached to the bones. Another job which the forelegs do is to pull the pony forwards so that the hind feet can land in approximately the position vacated by the fore feet. Again the knee is straight so the pull must come from the shortening of the shoulder muscles.

This implies that the fore must be lifted out of the way promptly to make way for the hind, another job for the muscles and tendons.

When viewed from the front the forelegs should not be too close together at the top ('coming out of one hole'). The knees should be the same distance apart as the fetlocks and feet so that the weight is carried symmetrically on the joints. The toes should point straight in front and look a perfect pair. Viewed from the side, the knee joint should be straight: being 'over at the knee', i.e. having the knee slightly in front, is a sign of wear caused by shortening of the tendons behind the leg; but the opposite condition, 'back at the knee' is a conformation fault regarded as much more serious. Remember, the forelegs take the strain with the knee straight both

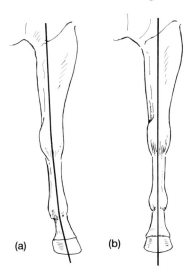

Fig. 4.7 Foreleg viewed from the front. (a) Bent – this fault imposes considerable stress on the tendons around the joints and uneven pressure on the articulating surfaces. (b) Straight – the fetlock joint should be straight above the centre of the hoof, and the knee straight above the fetlock. Make sure that the pony is standing correctly before you assess him.

Fig. 4.8 Diagrams showing how the forelegs take the strain during jumping and galloping. (a) Jumping – the foreleg is taking the strain as the pony lands. (b) Galloping – the foreleg is about to propel the pony into the suspension phase of the gallop.

when landing after a jump and when galloping, and this will cause an asymmetrical load if the leg is not quite straight.

The back

Presumably nature did not intend horses to carry the weight of a person, so having imposed this burden on him we should favour a pony with a strong back. For the length of the thorax (chest) and most of the abdomen, ribs are attached to the bones of the spine; these protect the delicate organs within the cavity and support the pony's spine, enabling him to carry weight.

A pony's back is like a beam supported at both ends by the fore and hind legs, and taking the weight of the rider. Unfortunately the beam has a weak point near the end, where there are no ribs. The longer the back, the more the bending moment, hence stress and strain on the spine. This is why a long back is weak. A word of warning: it is easy to wrongly think that a hunter's back is too long because his legs are short.

Compare Fig. 4.9a, a horse with a lot of daylight, whose back looks short, with Fig. 4.9b, a hunter with short legs, whose back looks long. There is an optical illusion here because the two backs are actually the same length. What really matters is how much unsupported spine there is.

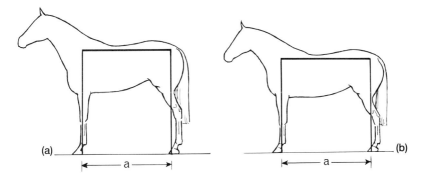

Fig. 4.9 It is easy to think that a hunter with short legs has a long back. Compare the drawings above: due to an optical illusion, horse (a) appears to have a shorter back than horse (b), but both backs are exactly the same length.

The usual test is to make a horse stand with his legs square and you should only just be able to lay four fingers on his flank between the last rib and the point of the hips; and there should be no more space than that. With a small pony there may be less.

Look for slackness in the loin. Figure 4.10 shows a weak back.

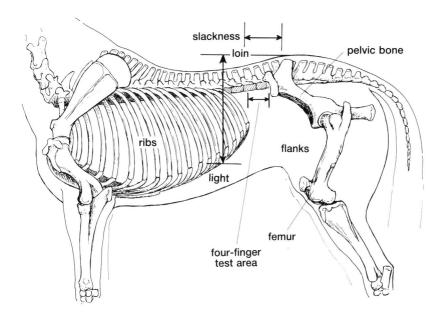

Fig. 4.10 The long, slack back (the four-finger test). There would be room for at least six fingers between the above horse's hip and its last rib. Compare this horse's frame with the one shown in Fig. 4.11.

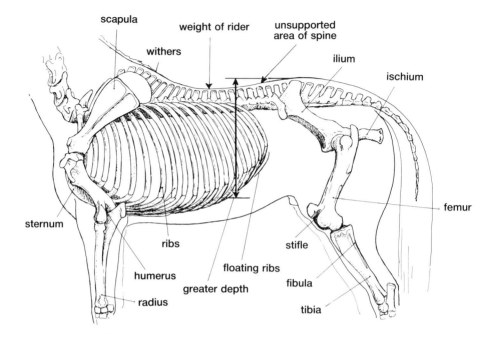

Fig. 4.11 A well-proportioned back.

Such ponies tend also to be shallow ('light through the loin'), to 'run up' when in work and to look 'herring gutted'. Thus it is difficult to make them look good in the show ring. Do not forget, short backs tend to go with short necks.

There must be room for the saddle without it sitting on the loins, especially if you want to ride side-saddle. We have heard it said that brood mares are preferred with long backs to make room for the foetus. That sounds suspiciously like an idea expressed by someone breeding for in-hand classes; in our view ponies are intended for riding, and any in hand showing must be a means to an end, namely producing a riding pony and not an end in itself.

Do not expect short-backed offspring from long-backed mares; this is not logical or reasonable. Anyway, a brood mare with a short back will be able to push her foal into the world more easily than will a long-backed mare because the former's muscles are short, not long and weak. As with most points of conformation, moderation is the order of the day.

An interesting feature of pony conformation is that the bones of the forelegs do not connect to the spine except by soft tissues. The vertebrae, the individual small bones of the spine, carry vertical members like bony fingers pointing upwards, known as spinal processes. These are used to attach the muscles which articulate the legs, so they are very important. The spinal processes are of different lengths, the longest forming the withers. A well-formed wither is a strong attachment for the muscles of the forelegs. A good length of wither is desirable as well as a good height.

There are important muscles, too, along either side of the spine and running along its length. In a pony which is 'let down', i.e. not working-fit – or badly ridden – these muscles are less apparent. They are frequently absent in a pony experiencing pain from back trouble; they affect the fit of the saddle. A pony which is schooled to hold its head and neck in the correct position and to move well, will develop these and other muscles, as will trotting uphill.

Muscles protect the spine from undue strain so it is sensible to improve your pony's fitness, which is a gradual process, before giving him strenuous work.

Thus the backbone (spine) is of great importance to the structure of the pony. Fortunately its conformation can be assessed very quickly by looking at the top line viewed from the side. It is defined by the shape and length of the spinal column and how this is furnished with muscle and fat. The correctness of the spine depends on the balance of the pony and on the correct positioning of the other bones of the skeleton.

If the spine is too short then the back and neck will be short, and this gives rise to problems. A short neck predisposes to lack of flexion, thickness through the jaw line and therefore wind problems. A short back, though very strong and useful for pulling loads, is not a good riding back. Room is needed to position the

Fig. 4.12 Slackness over the loin. The area behind the saddle and in front of the croup is hollow. The use of a numnah can sometimes indicate that the wearer suffers from back trouble.

saddle correctly with the arch sitting behind the shoulder blade. If there is lack of room here, the weight of the rider will be too far back, possibly pressing on the weak part of the loins and over the kidneys. Or, if the saddle is too far back and the pony bucks, the punch of the hind legs will be felt very strongly through the seat of the rider, who is likely to be pitched forward and off.

Any fault in the spine will predispose to unsoundness and no amount of corrective measures and good riding will be of long-term good. If the pony is stronger on one side than the other, and this is often the case to some degree, it will be a constant battle for the rider to keep him straight between hand and leg. Sloppy riding can also be a cause of incorrect top line shape and efficiency, and must be avoided. It is very important that a rider understands how to keep a pony straight by using his hands and legs, because it is in this way that the pony tracks up properly in two tracks only. If the pony moves in more than two tracks, then he will twist his spine and be crooked. In turn, this type of movement will make the muscles develop unevenly on each side and the pony will find it very difficult to accomplish anything but the simplest movements. This is one way in which riding affects the conformation of the structure of the pony.

Bone, substance and quality

We need some means of accurately assessing how substantial a horse or pony is in relation to its height.

One way would be to weigh the animal, but this is of limited value, for a horse which carries a lot of fat might have a heavy top, and we are not particularly interested in the flesh in this connection, rather the framework.

Another method used by carters of old was to measure the distance round the girth. This gave a crude assessment of heart and lung room, quite useful because it gave a measure of the ribcage (plus any layer of fat and muscle), essentially the framework. This is interesting because one can now obtain tape measures calibrated in pounds and kilogrammes, to put round the girth, which again provide a measure of weight.

The above method suffers in that it measures only the body of the horse when it is really more important to measure the legs. A heavy-topped horse on light legs has bad conformation.

Consequently, to assess the horse's 'bone' it has become practice

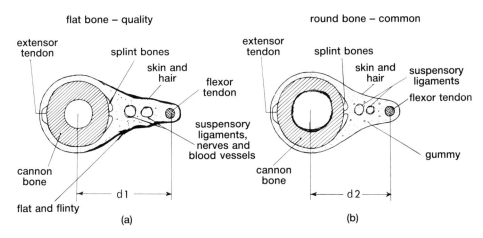

Fig. 4.13 The measurement of bone – i.e. the distance round the leg below the knee – is the same in (a) and (b), but these cross-sections through the cannon bone reveal that the distance 'd1' is greater than 'd2' and therefore gives more leverage to the flexor tendon in flat bone.

to measure the circumference of the cannon bone below the knee. It should be borne in mind, though, that this measurement includes not only the cannon bone but also two splint bones plus several tendons, suspensory ligaments, blood vessels, skin and hair. Usually it gives an indication of the leverage of the tendon, shown by the dimension *d* in the Fig. 4.13. A large distance here implies good conformation; it features what is known as 'flat bone', a curious term, but one which is important to understand. If the cannon was slightly larger then *d* would be less for the same bone measurement. This is known as 'round bone' and is not such a strong conformation as 'flat bone' because the tendons have less leverage.

If the sides of the lower leg are hollow rather than 'gummy' or puffy, so that the outline of the suspensory ligaments can be seen under the skin, this is known as 'flinty' bone and is regarded as desirable.

So in quality legs look for:

- big bone measurement below the knee
- flat bone
- flinty bone
- plus the other desirable features previously described

Longclose Guilthwaite. Although a little thick under the neck and with slightly sickle hocks it is nevertheless a good stamp of hunter pony, and, though aged, is still sound. Other good features: quality legs, strong forearm and second thigh, deep body, good length of rein and correct pasterns.
(Photo: J. Thorne)

Overall quality requires quality legs plus:

- a good hunter head, neither too large or common, nor too small and pretty
- a good front and depth of body
- balanced overall conformation

Substance implies:

- big bone measurement as above, plus adequate width, neither too narrow nor too wide
- strong natural muscle development, especially of the forearm, second thigh, quarters and back. (NB: A pony with natural well-developed muscles will have these on his forearm and second thigh even when he is let down and not in work.)

CHAPTER 5

Buying and Selling

BUYING

When buying young unbroken or broken but untried ponies it should be remembered that the risks are quite high, for the pony may never become a good performer. Firstly young ponies are susceptible to all kinds of ailments and setbacks, such as splints, spavins and wolf teeth; mares may experience ovary problems, and at worst colts can die after gelding. These are only a few of the hazards.

Older ponies will have gone through most of these phases, and will either have come through sound, or not. So the older pony, if he is sound, will probably be a better proposition, unless you have lots of time or you have lots of your own ponies to choose from.

People who buy a fleet of four-year-olds regularly, must expect a fairly high rate of disappointments. Apart from the aforementioned problems, there is no guarantee the ponies will jump well. In our opinion people who buy youngstock, however well bred the animals are, have no assurance of eventual success. Bear this in mind when considering price.

It is not advisable to pay too much for potential; it must also be realised that a good jockey is a must. Some exhibitors have one good pony after another, and when it does not perform as well as it should, they blame the pony when really the jockey is at fault.

As an analogy, take the yearling sales at Newmarket. Every year record prices are paid for well-bred stock, but how many of these actually win a race? In fact only one in ten horses purchased in this manner ever win a race, even a minor stakes. However, people continue to buy yearlings because the potential rewards and excitement are enormous; we all hope that one day we will buy a Mill Reef.

With ponies the stakes are lower because the financial rewards bear no comparison but the disappointments and frustrations can be equally acute, especially for the younger rider.

There are many ways to go about buying a pony, and we all have our favourite methods. You can buy from a dealer if you know one well, but make sure you understand the deal. Obviously some dealers are excellent, but a few let the side down by sharp practice.

Another way to buy is from a farmer's wife; many breed a few ponies as a hobby and some have very nice animals to offer.

You may wish to buy from a riding school because your child likes a certain pony and has got used to him. However, this may not work out very well because a riding-school pony may behave very differently when taken to a private home. Here he may not have enough exercise or may miss his friends; he may even miss the confines of an indoor school or manège and go quite potty in the open.

To buy from a private home often works well because you may have a chance to watch the pony at show or even to ride out with him.

Answering advertisements can put you under pressure to make up your mind quickly. But at least the advertisement will include some description of the pony, and by law the advertisement should be honest and fair or the vendor may end up in trouble.

Alternatively you can study prospective ponies at larger shows, which will give you a fair idea of their capabilities and manners. At the BSPS championship show, ponies that are for sale are marked as such in the catalogue. This does, however, put a great strain on their jockeys as they know that people are watching for this purpose.

Another good way to buy is to advertise in the 'Wanted' column of horsy magazines or local papers. You may receive some very strange replies, but at least you will not be in competition with other buyers so time will be on your side. We have bought several ponies this way and it has proved a very satisfactory method.

A good time to buy is in the autumn because you will have lots of time to get used to the pony before the open season. However, if the pony is to be a novice, then you may prefer to buy it in the spring.

It is sensible to make a list of exactly what you are looking for so that you do not get side-tracked. Size and price, age and experience are very important, so make sure you have all these details before you set off to view a potential purchase.

If you expect to buy a three- or four-year-old that has been backed and quietly ridden away, that is calm and confident with people, and that is traffic-proof as well, you must be prepared to pay a reasonable price for such a nicely brought on pony. To produce a pony to this level takes a lot of time and trouble.

If you are prepared to take a risk and like a bit of excitement you could buy a pony at an auction sale (not a route for the fainthearted). Remember that sales have fairly strict codes of practice and print their conditions of sale clearly in the catalogue. Read them carefully so that you fully understand the small print. Go through the catalogue before the sale, select a few ponies that may be of interest and go and look at them. Ask the vendors lots of questions, if they are there, and write down what they say. Take a witness with you.

We recommend that you bid only for a pony that is fully warranted according to the conditions of sale – and make sure you know how long the warranty lasts. Do not have the pony vetted at the sale; take him home to get to know him a little, then have your own vet give him a thorough examination at home. Don't skimp on the vetting: have the feet x-rayed and the pony's blood tested if you have any qualms. If the pony does not come up to his description, inform the auctioneers at once and return the pony to the saleyard immediately, with a written explanation of the reason for return. This must be done within the time stipulated in the catalogue.

We have bought nine horses at saleyards and they have all been satisfactory except one. This was returned under warranty, and there were no problems. One of the most successful sale buys was a black four-year-old pony; we still have him now, in very good form, at twenty-one.

Whatever the method of purchase, take your time, it is not wise to rush into buying. Never be bullied by the vendor, who might tell you that someone else is interested and therefore you should make up your mind. In these circumstances it is better to withdraw and go back later if the pony is still unsold. Remember: 'Buy in haste – regret at leisure'.

AGE CONSIDERATIONS

The age of the pony you buy very much depends on your own choice, the ability of the rider and the class you wish to enter. At one time only young ponies were considered to be in the running for winning a class. In the early days, all WHPs were judged by show pony judges. Since many of these were breeders and therefore used to having young ponies around them, they tended to favour the younger entries. However, it became apparent that a WHP was not ready to do well at a young age – he needs time to gain experience – so gradually the merits of the older pony were recognised.

We have come to the conclusion that ponies of four, five and six years of age are frequently mentally immature, so if you choose to buy one of these 'adolescents' you must be prepared for the ups and downs, and have the experience to cope with 'teenage' problems.

The idea of a schoolmaster for a young child is a sensible one: a young or novice rider needs the confidence that an older, experienced pony can give. Also, a young child cannot successfully educate a young pony unless that child has learnt from an experienced pony and knows what to do, especially when things

Lynscott Medallion, owned by Mr and Mrs Brown. Only 13.0½ hh and a small supreme winner, in 1978. (Photo: *T. Wilder*)

go wrong. Only consider a young pony when your rider knows how to ride a novice; he will need to be patient, knowledgeable and skilful.

Sometimes a four- or five-year-old pony will qualify for the open WHP class at the championships, but it may be too early to take him round the course. By all means enter him in the catalogue, so you can demonstrate that he has qualified, but consider very carefully whether you want to put him into the class. If you bring him back a year or two later, he'll be able to tackle the job with more confidence, having more experience under his belt.

A word of warning: parents should not feel that they are buying success if they buy an older pony. The pony will only continue to do well if he is well ridden, and most competitors realise this.

To sum up, probably the best age for a WHP is eight to ten years old – he is mature, proven sound and consistent. But do not be afraid to buy an older pony – good ones seem to go on for ever.

An SHP is a different proposition. He does not need such a wide education and experience; he can therefore be shown when quite young and remain a good pony for a very long time, so long as he stays sound and relatively unblemished.

SIZE OF PONY

Again, there are many considerations. Try not to over-horse your child, or he may find he cannot get the best out of his pony. The pony will soon know that the child is too small and may take advantage, which can be very off-putting for a young rider.

A word about the size of the pony in relation to the class: if we are talking about WHPs then don't worry if your pony is a little small for the class. If he is good, he will qualify for the championships. At the championships the ponies are not usually seen together, but are judged individually, and by the time the ponies are brought to the final judging, the marks have been awarded. This is borne out by the fact that on several occasions small ponies have done well at the championships, e.g. Beckfield Ben Hur, who was champion, must have been well below 13.2 hh; another pony was Tonto, who was 13.1 hh. As long as the pony has the ability to jump the course, don't worry about his size. Lyndscott Medallion was also a very small pony for his class, and he won several times.

Tonto – supreme winner in 1970, owned by Mrs Bucknall. Again, small for his class, but he made up for this in ability. (Photo: Peter Rollinson)

VETTING WHEN BUYING

Whether or not you have a prospective new pony vetted is entirely your decision. However, if the pony is to be insured then the insurers will probably require a veterinary certificate of soundness before they will take on the risk. The rules will vary from company to company.

Even if you are having the pony vetted solely for peace of mind, you need a clear idea of the main areas of concern.

You will need to ask the vendor pertinent questions about the pony's health and behaviour: do not be afraid to do this because the vendor has, by law, to stand by his word. Do ask if the pony receives any additives or drugs and if he is warranted sound: ask if he is easy to catch etc. Don't be satisfied with an assurance that you needn't worry about such things. Take a witness with you and be suspicious of evasive replies. Make notes.

Tell your vet exactly what you want to use the pony for. This helps him to assess whether the pony is sound and suitable for a particular job. Certain qualities will be imperative for your needs whilst others may not matter. When you first try the pony make a mental note of anything you notice which worries you so that you can tell your vet to pay special attention to these points. If

Fig. 5.1 Before buying a new pony, you may wish to have him vetted thoroughly. This will include a check on his heart and an examination of his eyes.

the pony is of considerable value you may wish to have his feet x-rayed and/or a blood sample taken. This sample does not need to be analysed straight away, but can be tested at a later date, if there is any dispute between you and the vendor.

If you cannot employ your own vet, try to find one who has not seen the pony before and is not employed by the vendor. Try to arrange to be present at the examination so that any queries can be dealt with there and then. If you feel the vendors are thoroughly trustworthy, as most of them will be, it may not be imperative for you to be present. But if you are keen on the pony but have some nagging doubts about the owners, then do go – and turn up early! A thorough vetting can take one and a half hours and is really worthwhile.

If the pony lives a long distance from your home and you feel unable to travel, you could ask your own vet to suggest another in the pony's area. Make the necessary arrangements by phone, specifying which vet you want for the job, then confirm the request in writing. If you have any particular worries about the pony, for example concerning a blemish, or the pony's exact height, you can include these in the letter and ask the vet to come back to you on these points. If he does not carry out your particular wishes you should query it.

If you send a general request to a veterinary surgery asking for a pony to be vetted, it is not automatic, unless you specifically demand it, that the best horse vet from that practice will be sent. A general vet, who does not specialise in horses, may not necessarily be adequate for you when buying a really special pony.

Also, do bear in mind that a vet can only act for one party. If a seller suggests that he is happy for you to contact his own vet regarding the pony's history, remember this vet's first loyalty is to his existing client. Very likely he will say he sees so many horses and ponies that he cannot possibly remember the one you describe. If he were to tell you something detrimental about the animal, he could lose the future work from that seller's yard – and the seller knows this. Therefore, this apparent recommendation is really of no value at all.

VETTING WHEN SELLING

You will obviously wish to present your pony in the best possible light so do make sure he is well groomed and his feet are picked out and washed. Be present yourself when the buyer's vet comes; it is not good manners to leave the pony in the charge of a groom who may or may not be able to answer the vet's questions.

Advise the vet at the beginning of the examination of the pony's present state of fitness, e.g. very fit, quite fit, just up from grass, etc. This will help him to evaluate the condition of the pony's heart and lungs.

Try to answer all his questions truthfully and helpfully. Evading questions or offering excuses will tend to make him cross or suspicious.

If you really care about the prospective home of the pony and are anxious that the pony will be too much for its future jockey, it may be wise to tell the vet. You will be upset if things go wrong after the sale and the pony has to be sold on again soon. With a little more time and patience you will be able to find a more suitable jockey. The buyer's vet may be able to reassure you, however, that the jockey does have suitable help and will be quite capable.

No pony is perfect, though some people and vets do expect them to be so. If the vet is unduly rough or inconsiderate in his examination, expecting too much fast work for which your pony is not fit, do not be bullied. If you have been fair and honest you are quite entitled to ask him to leave your home before any damage is done.

VETTING A PONY YOURSELF

If you know what to look for you can examine a pony yourself before having it formally vetted. This may help you to eliminate the pony, making a vet's visit unnecessary.

Things to look for

Look inside the pony's mouth and estimate his age by examining his teeth. There are many textbooks which have diagrams to help you learn this art. Check that when his mouth is closed the teeth meet correctly; particularly that the front teeth close perfectly together, neither being over-, nor undershot. An overshot jaw, called a parrot mouth, is hereditary and can interfere with the correct mastication of food. If the front teeth do not mesh, then the molars are not likely to either, and this will cause problems. Ponies' teeth continue to grow, unlike human teeth, and must have another tooth to grind against.

Feel down the pony's mane at the roots of the hair. If this feels rough, ask if the pony has had sweet itch. This again is hereditary and very unsightly in the show ring. Look at the wither area for signs of pressure from tight-fitting rugs and saddles. Some ponies are more prone to sores than others, presenting problems with tack and clothing.

Feel down the spine on both sides. If the pony flinches he may have spinal trouble, or muscular problems. If so, he may need help with his back to put it right and this may be an ongoing problem.

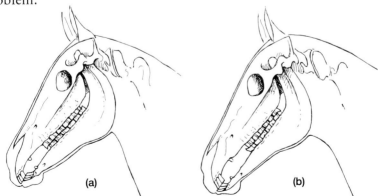

Fig. 5.2 The pony's jaw. (a) Overshot – parrot-mouthed. (b) Undershot.

Check over the legs minutely, examining for blemishes, bursal enlargements, and thickness of the tendons. Any tendon enlargement will almost certainly lead to trouble in the future.

Feet are obviously very important. Distinctive faults are: narrow, boxy feet; spread, flat feet; lack of frog; dropped sole; long heels on the hoof; damage to the coronet area; and severe ridges on the hoof, which may indicate laminitis.

Look carefully in the hock area for bone spavins, bog spavins, and curbs. Check that the hind and front legs are pairs – look from behind, in front and from both sides. Look at the hips: they must be absolutely level.

Generally the pony should look correctly proportioned, e.g. the head must not be too small or too big for his body; the front of his body should match the hind. He should not be overtopped or his legs will break down under work. He should not be shallow in his body as this means he will not have enough heart or lung room. If he is too narrow he will lack stamina. Whatever type he is, then each part of him should echo this type.

If there is undue wear in the joints this will be evident; they will be knobbly and possibly not pair up with the other leg. This can be found even in a very young pony, either because he has had too much work too young or because he has inherited a tendency to weakness in the joints.

Observe the pony's surroundings. Look at his stable carefully as you go in. Are there chewed doors, anti-weaving devices, kick marks on the walls, etc.? Is he the culprit? Also look at the field in which he has been living. Is it full of weeds? Beware, especially if you see ragwort. If he is still hot from just being ridden, maybe it was done to loosen him up before you arrived, so that he goes sound for you. If you arrive early you may catch the vendors redhanded; and even giving him an injection. Be suspicious: if you buy a used car with a faulty part, a new piece can be bolted on; but if you buy a broken-down pony, it may only be fit for the butcher.

This thorough check-up is really worthwhile. If you can take a more experienced person with you, you will learn a great deal and could be saved a lot of problems, time and money. You would be vexed if the vet found something blatantly wrong which you could have spotted yourself.

Have the pony trotted up for you to see if he is level and sound; also that he moves straight. A show pony must move straight and in strict time depending on the pace. There should be no signs of forging, or knocking himself. Look at his legs for evidence of these problems. The wear on his shoes can tell a story; the shoes should be quite level and evenly worn.

Having decided that you like the pony, you must decide whether to have it vetted. Remember, you cannot check his eyes nor his heart; nor may you spot, for example, a shiverer or a pony with stringhalt.

GETTING USED TO A NEW PONY

When a child moves up to a new pony a certain amount of patience is needed, because the best results are not usually obtained immediately. It can take up to six months for a partnership to develop into a first-class combination; it may take longer, so be patient. Occasionally things click quickly, and some riders are particularly talented, but it is not the norm.

Let us look at the fundamentals involved, and ask ourselves why a pony behaves as he does while ridden. He is not a machine and can only obey an instruction when he understands what is being asked. Therefore he must learn a language. But your language may not exactly match the one he was taught by his previous jockey. Hence the need for patience while rider and mount get to know one another.

SELLING

When the time comes to sell your pony, do not make the mistake of selling him too soon. If he is going well, is not too small for your jockey, and they are still in the class, they may as well stay together as long as possible. It is not easy to find a replacement, and one more year is not likely to make much difference to his price.

CHAPTER 6

Early Training

MANNERS

Training should begin when you first bring your pony home into the yard. The way he responds to you and vice versa will deeply affect his behaviour and eventually his performance in the show ring. It is a good idea from the outset to make it quite clear to him what you expect at all times. For instance, when he is turned out in the field, he must not be allowed to barge or push you over. He should stand quietly while you undo the gate and release the headcollar.

These details matter. When you are with him in the stable he should behave himself at all times, standing still while you attend to him. He should mind his manners with the blacksmith, the vet, or indeed anyone who has to handle him. If, when he arrives, his manners are less than perfect, identify the problems and try to correct them one by one. A horse or pony is a single-minded animal and cannot cope with more than one lesson at a time.

Whenever he is saddled up ready to ride, the first thing you must insist upon is that he is obedient and stands rock still while your jockey gets on board. If he moves, the jockey should dismount and keep trying until this is achieved. If necessary, offer the pony a few titbits while your jockey mounts to distract him from his bad habit. He must learn to stand and wait until his rider is ready to move off. Obviously the jockey must be trained in these good habits too. These basic lessons make for good manners and safety. The good habits which you are hoping to establish must never be allowed to waiver; they must be a matter of routine. This helps the pony to feel secure and happy, and forms a sound basis for further training.

Sometimes you will have to be very patient, but by watching your pony's reactions you'll soon be able to judge what he is thinking. Ears that are continually flicking forwards and backwards show that the pony is listening and trying to understand; if they stay lying backward, then the pony is resisting, cross, or just plain awkward. Honest eyes are the ones that show no white, are usually large, and look interested. If the tail is clamped down, the pony is probably frightened or afraid of being chastised; if the tail is pointing to the heavens, then watch out for high spirits. However, if the tail is being swished round and round, then you have a real 'try-on' on your hands. This will probably be seen in a battle of wills. Be very calm and determined, and be prepared to spend hours if necessary: expect and get obedience. The pony's most honest expression is a big sigh, and is usually a sign that he has decided to give in.

THE WHOA

We tend to spend a great deal of time teaching our ponies to go forward, but it is also important to teach them to stop. The time to start is when your pony is very young, or as soon as you acquire him. Lead him about and keep asking him to whoa, and insist that he does so each time. When he is being turned out, say, 'Whoa' to him and make him stand still while you remove the headcollar, then give him a titbit and send him away.

Although titbits are not generally a good idea, they can be useful in encouraging the right response in training. You never know when you will need your pony to stop in a dangerous situation, so it is up to you to see that the pony knows how to, and does, stop when required. If you have to resort to titbits to achieve this, so be it, provided you use them in moderation.

BREAKING – THE BASICS

You may prefer to send your pony away to be broken if you do not have the time, the facilities, the experience or the patience to do it yourself. Choose your trainer carefully through personal recommendations, and having chosen him, trust him and take a close interest in your pony's progress.

Supposing you have a young pony who is completely untrained – where do you begin? Let us assume he will lead from a headcollar and is three to three and a half years old. We will also assume that he has had no frightening experiences and therefore is not afraid of people. The first thing to do is to handle him a lot. One way to do this is to bring him into the stable every night, groom him gently, talk to him, pick out his feet, and handle him all over, especially in the areas where his tack will touch him. When he is used to all this, lay a folded soft rug over him and gently unfold it down his back, do it up at the front, and make a fuss of him. Now place a roller over his back and do it up loosely. The second time you do this try doing up the roller more tightly, just enough to keep the rug in place. At this stage it can be left on all night.

If the pony is happy so far, it may be a good time to introduce the feel of a simple bit, e.g. a rubber snaffle. Initially this could be attached to his headcollar. Smear a little honey on the bit, gently slip it into his mouth and attach it to the headcollar with string. It helps to have an assistant to do up the other side. Leave him to chew his bit for fifteen minutes, then remove it.

Repeat the exercise over the next few days, then attach a side rein to each ring of the bit. The reins should be fairly heavy but loose, and buckled on to the roller. He will feel the weight of the reins and accept them by picking them up with his bit, and he will get used to the feel as being similar to a rider holding them.

Now he has learned two things: the feel of the girth around his middle, and the experience of having a bit in his mouth. This is quite a lot of progress and it may take two to three weeks to achieve. However, it is important not to hurry this stage as it is the foundation of all the work to come.

If all has gone to plan he may now be led out with his roller on, either in the field, or with another person out on the roads, as long as the road is a quiet one. He will not need his bit in for this but should be given it to chew on in the stable fairly regularly.

Before going further you will need access to a closed-in training area about the size of a dressage arena or a little smaller. It is always best to have an assistant during these early stages.

After being successfully led about, that is, without any fire-works or resistances, you can begin to walk him about in circles, gradually reducing these to 20 metres in diameter. Next day put on a lungeing cavesson instead of a headcollar. At first a lunge line can be attached to the cavesson underneath his chin, rather than on the front of the noseband. One person can continue to walk with him while the other gradually takes up a position in the middle of the circle. If he is good and takes this in his stride, make a fuss of him, take off his tack and turn him out.

The next lesson is to introduce a lunge whip, which should be carried unobtrusively. Don't forget to walk the pony on both reins and to use your voice to give commands and praise him. Ponies do like to please you, so if things go wrong, you can bet it is your fault.

Gradually introduce the commands of 'Walk on', 'Whoa', 'Stand' and 'Trot on', and with your companion's help and a gentle movement with the whip behind the pony, ask him to move forward at the pace required. Do this quietly on both reins. But, remember that the whoa must be established before anything else.

When the walk and trot are fairly established, a new piece of tack may be introduced: the crupper. Choose one that buckles on both sides of the tail. This will make it easier to put on. Adjust the crupper and attach it to the roller. This will feel strange for a day or two, so you may have to go back to gentle walkabout.

The next stage is to attach his bit to the cavesson so that he is now familiar with: a cavesson plus bit, a roller plus crupper, loose side reins, a lunge line attached to the cavesson, and a lunge whip being gently and unobtrusively held. Quite a lot for a young pony. He has come a long way in his education, and if all has gone well, you may wish to turn him away for a fortnight.

It does not matter if it takes you longer than a professional to break your pony. A well-trained, calm pony will be your reward.

LONG-REINING

Long-reining is a most beneficial part of training and can be started as soon as the pony is lungeing well and understands the trainer's commands. To prepare him for having a strap resting on his hocks, use a heavy-duty cord or leather strap in place of the normal fillet string on his rug, and let him get used to this in his stable.

Put on the lungeing tackle, using a roller with rings at the sides, about level with the pony's muzzle when he is carrying his head in the correct position.

With your assistant, take the pony to your training area, with the lunge line fitted as usual to one side of the noseband. Lunge him for a short while on both reins, then attach a second rein to

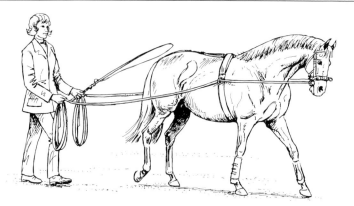

Fig. 6.1 Long-reining – a most useful training method.

the other side of his cavesson. Thread this through the ring on the far side of the roller and bring it over the pony's back, so that you now have a rein in both hands. Keep working on a circle, with your helper walking beside the pony.

Gradually come off the circle so that you are walking more and more behind him, and very slowly fade from his sight, until you are walking directly behind. When he is settled, let your helper also fade from his view, so that he is really on his own.

It may take the pony time to get used to the rein over his hocks, so be patient. When he is settled, start to introduce gentle turns to left and right, giving him plenty of voice aids. The beauty of long-reining is that he learns to take instructions from behind, which means that he is not going to be dismayed when you talk to him from the saddle.

Long-reining gives you a lot of control. If the pony refuses to go forward, you have the lunge whip to encourage him, if he wants to go too fast for you, you can turn him either way. But, ultimately, if you have already taught him to whoa, you should not have this latter problem.

If you have the energy you can take your pony for long walks about the farm, or on very quiet roads, with some help if needed. He can learn to stand still and wait patiently while, for example, you talk to a friend.

Long-reining can take a lot of time, but you will reap rewards in the future by having a more confident pony. If things go wrong at any time, you can resort to long-reining to calm him.

Having trained your pony to be driven in long-reins, you will be able to lunge him with two reins, the outside one going round his hocks. With the help of an assistant you can train him to turn towards the outside of the circle and then go round the other way. He will enjoy it. However, if you do this, you will not need to pass the reins through the rings of the roller.

BACKING

As soon as your pony is obedient on the lunge, without a helper guiding him, you can replace the roller with a saddle. An old one will do. When he is quite confident with this, he can have his first backing session.

Take the pony indoors and ask your helper to gently lie over his back, just a little at first, then gradually more. Pat him on the shoulders and continue until the right leg is put over the back. Take plenty of time over this. Many people prefer to back their ponies initially without a saddle and this is good practice.

When this is accomplished, take him outside to an enclosed area and repeat the procedure. If all goes well, he can be led about with his rider on board. Eventually the rider can take up the weight of the reins while the lunge line is slightly lengthened. So now he is nearly going with his jockey on his own. It is essential that the working area is quiet and free of distractions.

In the next lesson a schoolmaster could be ridden alongside the novice to give the youngster confidence. Soon the two ponies can be ridden quietly around the field, and later around the farm or quiet roads. Allow the ponies to take it in turns to go in front, and encourage them to pass each other without being upset.

Learning to trot with a rider must be done in a field, but if the lunge lessons have been done well, this should cause no difficulty. An occasional canter within the confines of the arena can also be tried – just a few strides to start with. When this is accomplished, the pupil is usually ready to go out on longer rides with his friend, and sometimes alone; he will also be ready to begin circle work to start his schooling for the ring.

SCHOOLING A NOVICE FOR THE RING

Your pony should learn to walk a figure-of-eight, then practise this at the trot. Make the circles large as he will not yet be balanced enough for small ones. When he is ready, he can canter these large circles, then come back to the walk and halt. He must learn to stand still until asked to move away. He will need to be trained to stand still while a judge handles him all over. He must also learn to run up in hand. All this must be perfected at home.

Whether you have been training your own young pony yourself or have just bought one, you will be wise to begin showing him a few times during the winter months at a show in an indoor school. This environment is ideal for a youngster, helping him to concentrate on his work. To start with you could enter him for show hunter pony classes or the novice show pony classes. Obviously he is not a show pony, but the experience of being ridden quietly in a competition will be good for him.

A young pony must not be hurried. If you rush his education you will regret it. After his first winter season it may be wise to give him a rest for a few months in the field; after all, he is still growing, and he needs a while to think about all the exciting things he has learnt so far. However, if he accepts his training with no set-backs, he can continue to be shown quietly in any classes which you feel are useful and novicey enough for his education. He can learn to jump at home and take part in a few minimus jumping classes.

At the beginning of his second winter indoor season he will be at least four and a half years old and, depending on his progress, may or may not be ready to be shown in qualifying classes. The BSPS winter season provides classes for show hunter ponies and novice working hunter ponies, so those who qualify in these events are eligible to compete at the BSPS winter championships held in the spring.

We would hope he will remain a novice throughout the following season because he will still be a young pony and should not be subjected to the higher fences of open classes nor the competition of the more mature ponies.

When the pony is still young, and in fact at all times when he is being ridden, it is most important that he tracks up. Tracking up means that his hind feet step into the prints of his front feet, so you will see only two tracks being made by the pony's feet. This will be very obvious on soft ground, sand or snow. If he is not tracking up, then he is not using his body correctly and evenly. He will move crookedly, be uncomfortable to ride, and be inclined to knock his own legs with his feet. As a result his muscles will develop more strongly on one side than the other. If he is always ridden with this problem in mind, and always persuaded to track up, he will be more likely to develop good straight movement and be a balanced ride. If you have problems in knowing if the pony is tracking up, ask an experienced friend to watch the pony's action and tell you if he is crooked. Then you will know how he feels, and be aware of the problem, and be ready to put it right.

Shaping up

The way you work your pony will make a significant difference to his shape and way of going. Look at dressage horses, at horses trained for Western classes, at well-produced show horses, and compare them. The same animal can do all these jobs, but he will look very different, because the work he does will develop different muscles. If you want him to look good in a show class, then you must develop the right muscles.

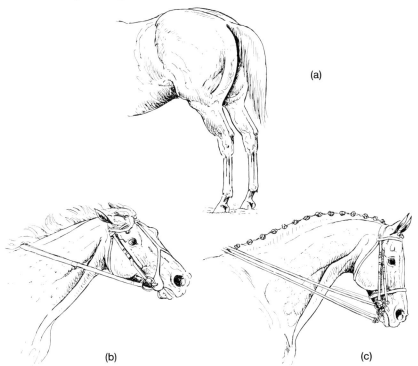

Fig. 6.2 Muscle development for different needs: (a) the Quarter horse; (b) the racehorse; (c) the show pony.

FLEXIBILITY IN TRAINING

There are no hard and fast rules when it comes to training a young pony, and you must be prepared to change your tactics for every pony as necessary, e.g. if your pony is frightened when being rugged up, start by using a tea-towel or something small until he is confident enough to have a larger item put on. If he will not tie up, you will have to spend time with him, holding the rope through a tie-ring until he stops protesting. As he pulls away, you can give and take until he is no longer upset and will stand quietly.

If traffic is a problem, then try tying him up where he can see traffic coming and going until he is used to it. He must obviously be in a safe place, and may need some soothing words. Sometimes it pays to give the pony his own way, until he is bored to tears with it, provided it is safe to do so. For example, if a horse decides to have some fun and take off with you, keep him going until he has had enough. Then, when he wants to stop, make him keep going. With horses you always have to use tact over strength, or brain over brawn.

Remember not to ask questions that your pony does not understand, and if during the training he does not comprehend, ask the question in a different way; e.g. if he will not jump a fence, do not struggle with him but let him follow another pony.

No book can cover all the aspects that a reader may need to know, so read as many books as possible. An excellent one on the training of the horse is *Equitation* by Henry Wynmalen (J.A. Allen), a most dedicated and gifted horseman.

To sum up one's relationship with a horse: 'Ask and he will give', 'Expect and he will try to give', but 'Demand, and anything or nothing can happen'.

THE RIDER

However well trained your pony is, your time will be wasted if your jockey does not ride well. The basic principles for a good rider are light and sensitive hands, and an independent seat. You cannot have one without the other.

Some people believe that good hands are born not made, just as some people have a gift for music. However, hands can be improved. The rider needs to know what he is doing and why. The hands hold the reins to guide the pony in the direction required, at the speed desired, and their aids must be given tactfully. If we are heavy-handed, the pony will lose his sensitivity. Therefore the lightest possible aids should be used to obtain the desired results. When a pony is being trained, the aids are usually quite strong, but as he begins to understand what is required, they can be progressively lightened. If a pony becomes insensitive to the hands, he will become 'wooden' and 'dead to the hand'. He will be difficult to ride, and you will have to go back to the drawing board and start retraining from scratch. If the mouth is damaged, this may be a waste of time.

An independent seat means that a jockey can ride without the need to hold on to the reins to support himself. To rely on the reins in this way sounds dreadful, but it is a fact of life for many unfortunate ponies. The rider must therefore learn to ride without reins. Years ago we were taught to blanket ride, i.e. a folded blanket was girthed on to the pony, and the pony was lunged with the rider in position. It taught the rider to balance himself, stay in the correct position without any help from the hands, and develop a supple, deep and strong seat. There was no help from a well-shaped saddle or stirrup irons. The result was to equip the rider with an independent seat and natural balance which would leave the hands free to be used with sensitivity, uncluttered with the weight of the body.

If a rider's hands are not independent this fact will manifest itself in many ways. One of these is standing up in the stirrups on the approach to a fence, just when the rider should be sitting firmly in position, and able to use the seat aids to push the pony forward into the jump.

So if your rider does not have an independent seat, you know what to do.

There is a saying: 'legs before hands', which means that the rider needs to create impulsion with his legs and seat, and then control the forward movement which has been produced, with the hands. This makes sense, and needs some thought. But even before the rider uses his legs, there must be contact from the hands. Many riders find it difficult to have the right amount of contact without holding too much or leaving the reins too slack. This is why it is so necessary to have an independent seat, leaving the hands free to give just the right amount of feel to the pony's mouth.

Only through the aids can we converse with the pony and

obviously if we use the wrong signal, we will not get the answer we expect. This can create frustration in a young rider, so we must teach him patience and equip him with knowledge; in the pony, however, the wrong aids can create confusion, and confusion leads to apparent misbehaviour – 'apparent' because the pony usually tries to understand what is asked of him and follow our instructions.

To sum up, we must accept that the independent seat is perhaps the most important requirement in a rider; it is a skill which takes time and experience to achieve, and demands that a rider be fit and have good balance.

Contact with the pony's mouth must always be there, otherwise he will be lost through lack of instruction, and may lose confidence. He will need the rider to help him through tricky situations, and give him just the right amount of feel to suit the situation. When things go wrong, a rider needs to solve the problem by giving instructions through the aids, perhaps to rebalance the pony or to steer him out of trouble. A rider needs to spend as much time in the saddle as possible to become fit and responsive to his pony's needs. An enjoyable way to do this is to go hunting or to take part in mounted games, which will speed up reactions, giving the rider confidence and courage.

It is not enough to ride only in the show ring because the rider will not have sufficient experience to cope with the situations that may occur. The pair cannot be expected to act as a partnership, with mutual understanding and confidence, and the rider who lacks time and experience in the saddle invariably lets his pony down in the ring. One often sees, for example, a rider send his pony forward to a fence, then slacken off the reins at the last minute. Contact is lost, conversation stops, and so, usually, does the pony.

Experience for the rider on several different types and sizes of horse and pony is very beneficial, particularly in coping with some mouths that may be soft and others that may be less responsive. When a rider has had plenty of experience he will learn to adjust. He will then inspire confidence in all the ponies and horses he rides, because they will realise that this rider will not hurt him. The pony will have the confidence to take hold of the bit and go forward without the fear of getting jabbed in the mouth.

Be patient with your jockey: to ride well is not easy. Try to put yourself in his place, and don't ask him to do anything you are not prepared to do yourself. If you do not ride yourself you cannot begin to understand the problems your jockey may be experiencing. If necessary seek help from someone who is a successful rider in the discipline you are trying to learn.

Your aims will be to acquire true paces, even cadence, true tracking-up, correct outline, obedience willingly and sweetly given, a happy pony and a happy comfortable rider. The correct outline may be the most difficult to produce, but you must attain the best the pony can give, taking into consideration his make and shape. This is where the skill lies: riding the pony to make the most of his good points, and lowering the profile of his bad ones.

CHAPTER 7

More Advanced Training for Rider and Pony

RIDING FOR THE SHOW RING

You can make an ordinary horse look a million dollars by the way it is ridden and produced; this is especially so if it has natural presence. It can beat a more correct animal which behaves badly, has no sparkle, and is ridden in an unprofessional manner.

The seat which your jockey has learnt at the riding school may be right for general hacking or dressage tests, but is unlikely to be the most appropriate for the show ring. If you are going to show a pony to its best advantage your rider will have to adapt his techniques. There is no need to abandon entirely what he has already learnt, but if your rider has not been trained in a showing yard, he will not know how to get the best out of your mounts in the show ring, nor how to ride according to the occasion. Take time off, go to the big shows to observe the professionals in the hunter classes, look at how they sit both in the ring and when warming up outside. Ask yourself what is the difference about how they sit. You must be open minded and very observant.

The rider will need to sit a little further back than in the classical equitation seat. With the weight further back, the front of the pony will lighten, and the hocks will be forced to move from underneath to support this weight. This will help the hind feet to track up with the fore limbs. The fact that the rider sits further back forces the pony to take the weight with his hind legs more positively.

SCHOOLING THE OPEN PONY FOR THE RING

By the time the novice pony has had a season in the ring he will have developed physically and mentally, sufficiently to be able to carry out a professional show in the open classes. As he gets stronger he can be ridden at home in a pelham to accustom him to the curb bit and he can be expected to work in very much smaller circles. This will neaten up his show. Soon he will accept a double bridle without any resistance; remember the snaffle rein raises the head and the curb rein lowers the head and asks for collection. Collection, impulsion and balance are the keys to a polished show, and are explained fully elsewhere.

The main objective will be the open championships in the autumn. There are novice classes at this show too, but the most prestigious ones are the opens, which need a very good and courageous pony, ridden by a jockey who is experienced. As stated earlier, it would be a mistake to enter these classes, even if you qualify, if you know deep down in your heart that your pony is not ready. It is a good idea at this stage to do something different, so why not take him Pony Club eventing in the early autumn? This will have several advantages. Firstly, it will give pony and rider a welcome change of atmosphere and competition, and secondly, it will help to get them both really fit. But, of paramount importance, the dressage will help settle the pony, and the cross-country will allow the pony to enjoy a vast array of different fences.

Balance

A pony is said to be balanced when his weight and that of his rider is so distributed over each leg, that he is ready to be obedient to the rider's aids at all paces. He will move his centre of gravity naturally to keep himself balanced, so it is important that the rider is sensitive to this need and does not work against him.

Collection

A pony is said to be collected when he raises his head and bends the neck at the poll, relaxes his jaw, shortens his body, places his hind legs well under him, is on the bit, and is ready to obey the slightest indication of the rider.

Note the phrase 'bends the neck at the poll'. This is very important. The bend or 'break' must not be lower down the neck. If this happens, the head will be carried too low, and possibly behind the vertical. You will see plenty of photographs of horses

Longclose Guilthwaite. This champion WHP, ridden side-saddle, shows what a pony and rider look like when well trained. The pony's ears indicate that he is attentive, he is obedient and he is tracking up. The pony is collected and full of impulsion, using his quarters and whole shoulder. Note the concentration of the pair – a sign of a good partnership. (Photo: J. Thorne)

where this is happening; usually it is due to resistance to the hands and it encourages the hocks to 'be left in the last county'. It nearly always happens in a snaffle bridle, where the pressure is on the corners of the mouth: the horse is trying to take the pressure on the bars of the jaw, which is more comfortable to him. A double bridle, with a Weymouth or a pelham bit, plus asking with the hands instead of demanding, will help to raise the head, and provide more comfort, and the correct flexion.

Impulsion

It is useful to understand the full meaning of impulsion. Impulsion is power, or potential power, and it comes from the pony's hindquarters. But it is not just power, it is power with a little

(a)   (b)

Fig. 7.1 (a) Uncollected. (b) Collected.

added sparkle. It is created by the rider's aids from the seat down to the lower leg and creates energy in the feeling of a coiled spring. The power and movement is propelled forward through the pony's body to his head, and is controlled by the riders hands, which give instructions as to direction and speed. Impulsion can be present at all paces including the halt.

Gredington Paladin showing true straight action, typical of an excellent WHP at the trot. (Photo: J. Thorne)

Concentration

It will be evident from these descriptions that a pony can only be balanced or collected if he is listening and concentrating. He will find this hard work. Do not overdo his schooling lessons. Between his lessons take him out for a hack, start to teach him to jump very small fences, and generally keep him happy, relaxed and calm. If at any time he seems to be a little stale, turn him out for a couple of weeks, then he will come back to his work fresh.

Transitions

Apart from being balanced a pony must learn to cope with transitions from one pace to another. If he is balanced he will find his transitions easier. Basically, all transitions should be so smooth that they are quite unobtrusive and this requires considerable ability and patience from the jockey. Remember to get the walk right first. This should be full of impulsion (but not hurried), covering a lot of ground with each step, be relaxed and have a swinging tail. The trot should follow very smoothly so the jockey must anticipate the new movement. Keep the trot smooth and fairly slow, but with loads of impulsion. The trot to canter transition, and all the downward transitions require the same treatment, and they do need perfecting. The pony will find his transitions easier if, at the trot, your jockey is careful to rise and fall on the correct diagonal. He should sit as the outside shoulder comes down towards him, or, put another way, he should sit when the inside hind leg is put down.

RESISTANCES

A remarkable number of ponies are naughty in the ring and show resistances to the rider's hands and legs. There are two common causes (assuming your rider is not at fault) which should be investigated: one is an uncomfortable mouth and trouble with the teeth; and the other is a problem in the back. The pony's teeth may need rasping because if they are not smooth they will cause sores on the inside of the mouth and cheeks. His back may have been damaged through careless mounting, i.e. the jockey pulling himself up and twisting the saddle and spine in so doing. If the rider always mounts from a mounting block this will never be a problem. Once a back is damaged it could be a nuisance for the rest of the pony's life.

Not only is the pony's owner disappointed if the pony is naughty in the ring, but also so is the judge. So many times a beautiful pony will come forward only to misbehave, which from a judge's viewpoint is very sad. Do not forget to feed the pony according to the work done and watch this carefully.

Naughtiness sometimes happens in the spring with geldings. They seem to sense that spring has arrived even before we notice it and they show this by high spirits in the ring. These will subside, but be tactful and strict while they last. Resistances can take place later in the season, say, in July, and this may be due to boredom of the show ring. If so, take a few weeks off if possible and hack around the countryside or do some completely different type of work; even a rest in the field can work wonders.

Nappiness is the most common type of resistance. The pony sometimes refuses to enter the ring and then engages in a running battle to return to the exit. Sometimes nappiness occurs at a fence going away from the collecting ring, after the pony has already jumped a few fences quite happily. It is important that the pony does not get away with being disobedient even at the expense of being disqualified from the competition.

Basically, he does not wish to go forward by himself into the ring to perform on his own, and no doubt he behaves in a similar way at home. When training him at home one of the most common causes of nappiness is allowing the pony to come back to 'mother' after schooling. This becomes a habit. Therefore when schooling, do not do this. At the end of work, turn him away from the 'home' gate and ride quietly round the paddock, halting in the centre. Pat him and dismount, and lead him home to his stable. In time, he will forget to nap. If not, the problem can be severe, and there are two ways of attacking it. One is active and the other is passive. The active one is for the rider to use voice, whip and heel to insist that the pony goes forward. When he does, he should be praised by patting him and using the voice. The change of disapproval to approval in the rider's voice can work wonders and the pony's realisation that he actually enjoys the approval part is a step in the right direction. The passive approach is for the rider to sit still, and make the pony stand for a considerable time. If he attempts to move, continue to make him stand. Do this as long as it takes to make him thoroughly bored and then he will probably go forward.

Praise him and repeat these actions for as long as it takes for him to realise that nappiness is not acceptable.

Nappiness is one way of refusing to accept authority. The rider's ability to be patient and persistent is a part of his mental superiority over the pony. However, ponies are not daft. They can soon learn that it is more difficult for the rider to insist on obedience at a show. If this is the case, go to a local show and take the pony into the minimus ring several times. This may help a great deal, particularly as the jockey will be less tense than in an important competition. Soon the pony will gain confidence and hopefully give up this annoying habit. Unless any tendency to nappiness is overcome immediately, you will always have problems with the pony. Going back to long-reining can help to solve nappiness.

One must expect young ponies to have strong instincts, like not wanting to leave the security of the herd, not wanting to approach strange objects (especially moving or strange ones) or suspicion of water. Since even a young pony is considerably stronger and heavier than you are, physical battles are not a good idea. Your trump card is your superior intellect. You will need a lot of ingenuity, so that obedience is learnt without direct physical confrontation.

The strong instincts referred to above can also be your greatest ally. The natural fear of such a suspicious object as a lunging whip enables you to make ponies go forward when they are napping on the lunge or on long-reins. You will need to use a firm authoritive voice at the same time; eventually the voice only will be sufficient.

When ridden, the other aids such as the legs, weight and possibly the whip, will supplement the voice. Ultimately, in an established partnership, much can be achieved merely by a slight shift of weight, moving the rider's centre of gravity. So the training of your pony will be a gradual progression, from using the natural fears to advantage, to obedience, induced by aids so subtle that they are hardly noticable to a bystander.

You can take positive steps to avoid nappiness, by helping the pony to overcome fear. Take him in-hand round the village; show him drains, bicycles, cars, tractors, plastic bags; speak to him calmly and reassure him. When he goes out for his first hack, he will already have overcome his fear of these objects.

Another useful method is to ride out with an old 'patent safety' schoolmaster to lead the way and set a good example.

Many ponies go through a stage of shying and this will

wrong   right

Fig. 7.2 How to cope with a shying pony.

continue into a well-established habit if not cured straight away. The causes are fear, over-freshness, or being startled. Shying on the road, particularly when passing stationary vehicles or road works can be cured by turning the pony's head away from the cause of fear, urging on with both legs, using the outside leg more strongly well behind the girth to stop the quarters from swinging out into the road. If there is something he refuses to pass, the rider should dismount and lead him. If the cause of shying is naughtiness because he is over-fresh, the answer is more work and less food.

Throughout the training, try never to ask the pony to do something when you instinctively know that he will not respond with obedience, e.g. when the pony is fresh or fretful, it is no good asking him to learn to stand still. Try to always treat him in the same way from day to day so he knows what to expect, and never tease him. Teasing is something that animals do not understand, and you may end up with a bad-tempered pony.

LEG YIELDING

Most showing people tend to regard dressage with a certain amount of suspicion, and as something to be left to the enthusiasts. However, there are occasions other than in the show ring when a well-schooled horse will be appreciated. One that will move sideways to order as well as forwards and backwards can be an advantage, even out hacking. Anyone who has had a leg nearly scraped off on a gatepost when riding an ill-mannered pony will understand why. At the least, your pony should be taught leg yielding. If he is to participate in Pony Club eventing, the ability to move him around accurately within a limited arena will pay dividends. A good dressage book will give you all the technical know-how but, explained simply, leg yielding means that the horse moves sideways from one of the rider's lower legs; that is, if the rider were to leave his right lower leg just on the girth and move the left lower leg a little behind the girth, with the correct use of the reins the pony should move to the right in a straight line. His head and body should still look forwards but his whole body will move sideways. If the horse is moving to the right the rider should just be able to see the bump of his left eye. That will indicate that the position of his head is correct; the neck bend to the left should be very, very slight. As he moves to the right his near fore and near hind will have to cross over the tracks already made by the off fore and the off hind and they will, in fact, cross over in front of these previously placed legs. The pony may well be a little stiff when first asked to do these sideways movements and he may find it difficult to understand what is being asked of him. Introduce leg yielding a little at a time, so as not to make the lesson unpleasant, and soon you will find that he becomes more flexible, more obedient to the hand and leg.

If you find that your pony has difficulty in learning the movement it can be very helpful for the rider to have an assistant on the ground. Choose a place in a yard or field where there is a high hedge or a wall, and decide which way you are going to ask the pony to go sideways. The rider should apply the correct aids while the helper stands at the pony's shoulder, on the side that is away from the direction of movement. All three should face the hedge or wall. The assistant can help by placing a hand on the shoulder and perhaps a hand gently at the top of the neck, and possibly touch the pony's foot with his or her foot. This will help the pony to understand what is required. When he does one, two or three paces successfully make a big fuss of him, give him a little rest, then ask him to do it again. Again lots of fuss when he has done it correctly and then try it in the opposite direction. He'll soon get the gist of it. The whole point of having a wall or hedge in front of him is to make it quite obvious to him that he is not being asked to go forward.

The use of the reins plays a large part in lateral movements, and they can be used effectively to control the quarters. This is achieved by using the direct rein and the indirect rein. The direct rein is used by one hand, supported by the other rein, to ask the pony to move in the direction of the direct rein: i.e. to move to the right, pressure from the right rein is applied to turn the pony's head to the right; the left rein must not be slack, but supporting the head so that the hands are together and both reins taut, otherwise the head only will turn, losing directional control.

The indirect rein is the one opposite to the way that you wish to go. It is used across the neck as in neck-reining. The direct and indirect reins are used in conjunction with each other to control the movement.

Using the direct and indirect rein to turn your pony requires practice but, once mastered, these aids can be applied to control the hindquarters. For example, to turn right and, at the same time, prevent the quarters from swinging out to the left, take a direct hold on the right rein and an indirect hold on the left rein, pulling this latter rein a little across the neck to the right and a little backwards towards and behind the wither. The effect is to ask the pony to move to the right, with both his fore and hindquarters. Try it on a left turn, too.

It is a useful way of asking a pony to move, and can give extra control on corners if he is inclined to swing his quarters out, or to become unbalanced approaching a fence from a difficult angle. Side-saddle riders have to use these aids to ask the horse to leg yield to the left because they have no leg aid on the right. It is called using the indirect rein in opposition behind the wither. It sounds difficult. It is not. It is fun, and ponies love doing it.

REIN BACK

Another movement which some people seem to find difficult is the rein back. This is necessary for the show ring to finish off a good individual show. The pony comes to a halt, is asked to go backwards a few paces, then forward a few paces and into a square halt. The rein back is something which must be taught at home and is well worth spending a little time on. Ask your jockey to shorten the reins, place both hands fairly low, and use the voice, saying 'back' whilst squeezing with the legs from the knee down. What the pony will probably do is be confused and try to go forward, which is why the rider has shortened the reins and lowered the hands. Or he may try to throw his head up in the air; but, again, this is combated by the lowered hands. Obviously, if these resistances are met, either he simply does not understand what you want or he'd rather not do it. Whatever the reason, an assistant on the ground is extremely useful.

Ask the helper to stand directly in front of the pony's nose, and talk gently to the pony to reassure him. The rider can then give the aids to go backwards while the assistant very gently touches each of the pony's front feet in turn with his toe. Once you feel he has got the idea, see if he can do it by himself. When he has done it correctly give him lots of praise. Later on, when he is being schooled in the field or out on a ride, ask his rider to rein back to see if the pony remembers his lesson. Again, lots of praise if he gets it right.

There is one important thing to remember when training a horse or pony to go backwards. Before being asked to go backwards he should be brought to a halt and given time to balance himself. A lot of people canter into a halt and suddenly ask the pony to rush backwards, which is not fair. He needs to put his centre of gravity back where it belongs and must be allowed time to think about each set of new instructions. Therefore he should first be asked to stand still and to put his legs square. Then the rider should make sure that the pony's head comes down very slightly and that he relaxes in the lower jaw. If instructions are given at this point, the pony will rein back very sweetly.

When the pony has gone backwards four paces, again, just give him a second or two to shift his centre of gravity before asking him to go forward and into his halt.

By now you will have gathered that something like eighty per cent of your schooling is not spent performing little circles and figures-of-eight in the field. Most of the 'trimmings' are dealt with in other environments, for example, out on rides and hacks and in the yard. It is really only the main structure of your show which needs polishing in the field.

PROBLEM SOLVING

There are many problems which can beset a pony in the ring and one of them could well be that he won't stand still when pulled into line. This is another thing which must be practised at home – and you must insist that it is done properly, otherwise this can spoil his show and upset your day. To imitate show-ring conditions, line up two or three other horses and place your pony in the middle of them. Tell your jockey to make the pony stand, and not to take 'no' for anser. When the pony obeys the rider should relax his hand, speak to him, pat him and tell him how good he is.

This is also a good opportunity to bring the pony forward out of the line-up, as if he is to be looked at by a judge. Ask a friend to act as the judge, and insist that your pony stands correctly while being handled and inspected. Do not let him move from that position until you give him permission to do so.

We had an instance of this with a new, inexperienced pony. In his first ever class he refused to stand in the line-up, wouldn't go backwards and forwards at the end of his show, and showed his nervousness throughout by shaking his head up and down. As we had plenty of time between his novice class and a later, open class, we were able to gently introduce these disciplines at the show. We tactfully taught him how to stand still and when he shook his head he received a little slap on the shoulder with the whip until he didn't shake his head any more. He was taught to stand still by walking a few paces, then being asked to halt and stand still for a few seconds, before going on again a few more paces, to repeat the process. Then we spent a little time teaching him to go backwards and forwards. This time was most rewardingly spent as he went forward into the open class which he won.

An awful lot of people waste their time doing absolutely nothing whilst waiting between classes whereas they could usefully be giving their ponies a little extra training. This is particularly beneficial because the pony learns to concentrate in a show environment.

After a show, when discussing the day's events, you are bound to have lots of ideas as to why certain things went well or badly. You will be able to work out a strategy for the next week or two to improve the pony and jockey for the next performance. It is not a good idea to go straight out to the field and start schooling all over again. The only justification for doing this is if the pony had a particularly bad experience over a fence and you want to restore his confidence by encouraging him to tackle a very low version of a similar jump, gradually building up the height and spread to match the one at the show. This will help him enormously and you will probably find that next time he comes across this type of fence his fears will have vanished.

If you rehearse your individual show too often, the pony will learn it by heart, and will anticipate it in the ring, e.g. moving short behind at the trot while waiting to be asked to canter. So practise the separate movements and transitions in isolation rather than riding through the whole show.

We work on the principle that whenever a pony is being handled or ridden, he must behave himself at all times, and it is up to the handler to be sure that he does. It means that he is safe to handle and to ride, and is never ridden in a slovenly manner. Thus he will always be tracking up, balanced, and ready for the next instruction; and as long as he can understand his instructions, he will be calm and sensible. The scatty pony is usually the one who does not know what to expect from his handler because his handler has been inconsistent or unpredictable in his behaviour, not really having a training plan. This does not mean you cannot have fun with your pony. Far from it. Lots of fun can be had going to gymkhanas and hunting, but a mad gallop out on a hack is not a good idea.

If you have bought a pony that has done a lot of in-hand showing you may be at a great disadvantage in the ring for two reasons. Firstly, he may be bored with the show ring; and secondly, he may have been led always from the same side, and this makes for a pony who twists his head round and fails to track up in his movement. Plenty of lungeing on the other rein, and careful riding keeping him straight will help, as will a rest in the field.

The above problems are often the result of incorrect running up in-hand, when the handler has held on to the pony too tightly, forcing the head to bend towards the handler. If this is a severe problem, put on a cavesson with a fairly tight noseband and fix a rein on to the offside, take this rein round the offside of the neck, through the rings of a breaking roller and back to your hand. Then you can teach the pony to run up in-hand using a free rein on the near side, and lots of control on the offside to help to keep his head straight. He will find this tiring, so do not do too much at once. However, he must learn to run up freely, otherwise the judge cannot see him moving properly, and he will not move straight.

Bear in mind when you are schooling your pony that he is not physically mature until he is about seven years old. Therefore do not ask too many questions too early or you will spoil him.

CHAPTER 8

Schooling Over Fences

If you have a young pony he will need to be taught to jump in good style. The first thing to remember is that schooling over fences cannot be hurried; it makes us very sad indeed to see so many young ponies being irrevocably spoilt by impatient owners greedy to enter competitions too soon. The raw material varies considerably of course, and what is right for one pony is not necessarily right for another.

On the whole, working hunter pony fences are not too high, and almost any pony can be taught to jump reliably if patience and tact are used. But once a pony has been frightened by being asked too much too soon, by rushing his training, he may never regain full confidence.

A pony which, by accident or design, has jumping in its blood and shows a lot of aptitude, will probably learn quite quickly. However, beware of any showing great early promise, as these are the ones that can be overfaced and then tire of the idea of jumping.

As in all aspects of schooling, a gradual system of approach is necessary. Start by introducing a little jumping in the normal schooling sessions and make sure that both pony and rider are enjoying themselves. Do this without over-excitement and keep going over the earlier easier lessons before giving the pony anything new to think about. Always finish the session on a good note, even if it means returning to a more elementary lesson and performing this well.

If, in learning, a pony does something twice, be it good or bad, he has almost formed a habit; thus, a bad habit can be formed just as quickly as a good one. Two of the worst habits to avoid are nappiness and rushing fences, and these must never be allowed to develop. If you proceed progressively, acquiring good habits in modest steps, carefully adjusted to suit your pupil, you will have no problems. But don't get over-confident and start to rush; if you

(ABOVE) *Lady Jane, owned by Mrs Jenkinson, a regular winner in 'battle'
with Catherston Telstar. A typical WHP 13.2 hh type.* (BELOW) *Spellbinder
– a champion WHP produced by the authors. An honest, brave pony. The
rider should be looking toward the next fence, not backward.* (Photo: *Eventer*)

do, you'll have upsets, which you'll regret.

Ideally you should have access to a fenced-in area, and you will require some simple jumps and a very competent, experienced rider with a secure seat, hands of silk, patience and bubbling with confidence which he can transmit to the pony. You will require exceptional ability to keep your own temper and to be calm in all circumstances. You must be prepared to take the education slowly and tactfully, establishing one lesson at a time, yet without inducing boredom. You will need a sixth sense to know whether you are being 'taken for a ride' or whether the pony genuinely does not understand what you are asking. One word of warning: if you cannot be sure never to lose your temper when things go wrong, then leave the job to someone else.

Nappiness in jumping, and rushing of fences are dealt with later in the chapter but you must be on the lookout for these habits right from the start.

MAKING A START WITH A YOUNG PONY

You should protect your pony's legs while he is learning to jump, not only to avoid blemishes but also to avoid the pain he may suffer if he hits a fence. Over-reach boots and tendon boots are a good idea.

Most ponies appear enthusiastic about jumping, which is a good start. The great secret is to give your pony plenty of confidence in his own ability. He must believe he can jump anything you ask him to. So only put him over jumps you know he can manage, so he can develop that all-important confidence. If you increase the difficulty so slowly as to make it almost imperceptible, he will hardly notice that he is progressing. The ability to jump the height and spread of novice courses will come surprisingly soon.

As with other aspects of schooling the method we recommend involves small steps, each step being a natural follow-on from the last already mastered.

Basically we start by teaching ponies to stretch themselves over low spreads comprising two parallel poles. Hunter judges like to see ponies making a long bascule so that they can accommodate any front ditches and readily adjust in flight to clear any unexpected back poles or ditches behind. We firmly believe that a pony should be taught to jump spread fences before asking for height;

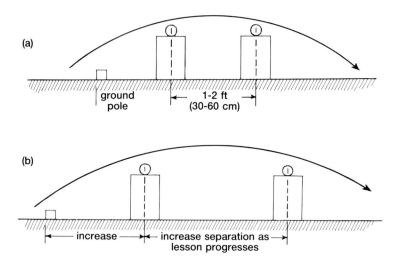

Fig. 8.1 Start each session with poles close together (a) and gradually increase their separation (b) as the lesson progresses.

he will take height in his stride when he is confident with depth.

Assuming that you have already taught your pony to pop over a pole on the ground or a low jump as a natural extension of his schooling on the flat, then place two poles on two 5-gallon (20-litre) oil drums (see Fig. 8.1), with one on the ground in front, providing a ground-line to help him judge where to take off.

For a start the oil drums need only be about 1-2 ft (30-60 cm) apart, and the distance increased gradually. Eventually they can be separated by as much as 6 ft (180 cm) for a 15 hh pony, but begin each lesson with the poles much nearer together than at the end of the previous lesson, and gradually increase again. This helps to remind the pony what you want him to do, otherwise he might get into difficulties trying to bounce the fence or drop a leg rather than keeping them both tucked up underneath him.

UPRIGHT FENCES

He will need to learn how to jump uprights, such as gates, planks or rails arranged in a vertical plane. If he is presented with this type of jump without suitable preparation he will not know quite what to do and may well try to take off in the wrong place or

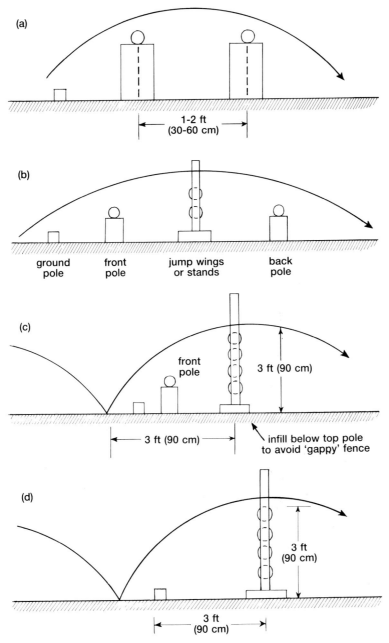

Fig. 8.2 Method of introducing or retraining a pony to jump upright fences.
(a) First, jump two low parallels. (b) Later, introduce a third, higher element
in the middle. (c) Remove the back pole. (d) Remove the front pole and
ultimately the ground pole.

perhaps 'cat jump' from all four feet at once. Either way he will lose confidence.

Again the training must be progressive. Go back and jump low parallels which he understands, and introduce a third element in the middle. This can usefully be a pole between a pair of standard jump stands.

As you will have observed, even without the new element, he will already be jumping surprisingly high at the mid-point in order to clear the back pole. The next stage is to remove the back pole and increase the height of the central element – and you are on the way to teaching him how to take upright fences.

If you watch novices you will notice that they frequently misjudge the take-off, either standing right back and jumping everything hugely, probably knocking off a pole with their hind legs, or alternatively getting right underneath, much too close, and knocking a front pole with their front legs. This can cause loss of confidence so it is important to help him initially. Although it will be necessary to remove the cavaletti, it is advisable to have a pole to indicate the take-off position.

To tackle an upright fence the pony will need to take off at a distance at least equal to the height of the jump, and Fig. 8.2d shows an arrangement suitable for a 3 ft (90 cm) high jump with a pole on the ground.

'CAT JUMPING'

This is a bad habit sometimes acquired by beginners; they take off abruptly, usually too slowly and without any impulsion. This at least exhibits a willingness to try, but it is uncomfortable, potentially dangerous, and not at all desirable. If you have proceeded along the lines which we have described your pony should not have acquired this habit, but if he has, reschool him over low parallels, for which a certain speed of approach is necessary, and then progress to ordinary fences with the bounce approach previously described.

When you have been through these procedures, which will take many training sessions of gradual progression, he will have to learn to jump an isolated fence, without the assistance of the cavaletti on approach.

Toyd Bewildered – supreme champion in 1979, owned by Mrs and late Mr T. Hunnable. The pony is jumping cleanly over a simple upright and looks happy in his work. (Photo: John Taylor)

SPREAD FENCES

The progression from low, deep parallels to higher ones with less spread is a natural one and if taken in small stages should not prove difficult for your pony.

Start with the low parallels as before then bring them nearer together increasing the height as you do so. At the same time introduce more poles below the front one, because a gappy fence is more difficult to jump. The pole on the back stand must always be a single one for safety reasons, and never lower than the top pole at the front. A pony needs to take off further away from a spread than from an upright. The rule is that the ground pole should be at a distance away from the jump equal to the height plus half the spread.

So for the example shown on a 30 in. (75 cm) high fence with

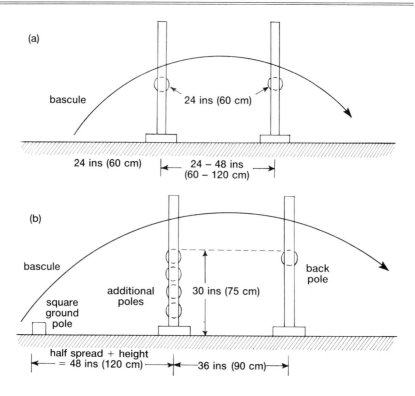

Fig. 8.3 Progressing to higher spread fences. (a) Start with low parallels as before. (b) Increase height, reduce spread and introduce more poles in first element. Ground pole distance = height of fence + half the spread.

36 ins (90 cm) spread the ground pole distance = 30 ins + 18 ins = 48 ins (75 cm + 45 cm = 120 cm).

'SEEING A STRIDE'

A pony's field of vision is quite different from our own and, in fact, nearer than a certain distance in front of a jump, he can no longer see the obstacle and has to jump from 'memory'. If he has a will to jump the obstacle, he will cope, jumping it fluently. But with a rider on his back, or with a reluctance to jump, he may be in difficulty. This is where a rider can help or hinder. If the jockey can 'see a stride', he will be able to give the pony the correct aid at the right moment for take-off. This is a great confidence-giver to the pony, and he will soon learn to trust his jockey to tell him what to

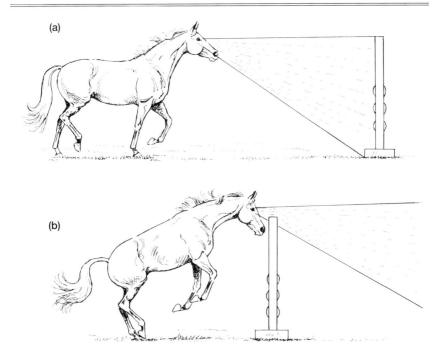

Fig. 8.4 The pony's field of vision when approaching a jump. (a) From here he can see the fence, by looking down if necessary. (b) By take-off time his head is raised and looking well above fence. If he looks down again at the last moment he will be unable to take off and will refuse the fence or plough through it.

do. A real partnership can be formed.

A jockey can learn to see a stride while on foot: watch the ground where you are walking, and try to imagine where each of your feet are going to step on the ground. You will be amazed at how accurate you can become at guessing. Another way is to place a stone on the ground and walk towards it, trying to guess which foot will be in the right position to kick it.

Now try to see a stride when on your pony, and when you have mastered this trick, you will be an effective rider over fences, sensing exactly where you will take off.

BEFORE COMPETITIONS

Before he is ready for competition two other aspects must be introduced. Firstly, variety. Your pony must learn to accept an

Five-year-old Spellbinder (left) is given confidence by twelve-year-old companion, Catherston Telstar. (Photo: J. Thorne)

infinite variety of fences: rustic, white, and coloured. If you have access to a novice cross-country course this is very good training; jumping with another older experienced pony to give him a lead is a good idea. Remember, at this stage you are teaching him to cope with all sorts of fences, not trying to push him to his limits. Use the course for practice – do not compete in hunter trials yet. Take each fence individually, make sure that it is not too much for him, show it to him and then let him jump it. Do this a second time, and a third if necessary. Reward him and go on to the next.

Before he is ready for his first novice WHP class he must learn to jump a course of jumps. The most important training in this respect is his work on the flat: if he has learnt to be obedient to the aids so that he can change legs at the canter and regulate his pace according to the wishes of his rider then this will come more easily to him.

The important thing is to approach each fence in a balanced way; and a competent rider is essential here. A careless rider who turns a pony into a fence short, and on the wrong leg, without giving him time to look at what is expected, is asking for trouble. An older, more experienced show-jumper might cope with this but a young WHP certainly cannot.

Your novice can be introduced to a course of fences, and to the atmosphere of a show, in a minimus ring. This will give you the opportunity to tackle a variety of fences without the pressure of competition. You can insist that he makes a good job of each fence before going on to the next.

It is very important that the first few shows you enter have flowing courses. Coursebuilders vary; some construct good fences but do not always position them well to form a good, smooth course. Look for courses with large sweeping curves. Know your coursebuilders and follow a good one.

During the course of your pony's jumping training keep up his other work, i.e. his schooling on the flat and hacking out. If on your rides you meet the odd fallen tree or ditch to pop over, or have to open and close gates, or go through water, these will all help his education. You may also be able to take him to a show, to experience the atmosphere and get him used to travelling.

The show hunter classes and unaffiliated show classes at local shows provide an opportunity for you to introduce your well-schooled pony to the show ring. They will offer a change of scene and add variety to his life. They may also have a minimus jumping class on offer.

Your practice jumps at home will probably be rustic, in which case do not forget to introduce white and coloured poles and wings. You do not want your pony frightened the first time he sees them at a show.

JUMPING PROBLEMS

Nappiness

Nappiness is rebellion against the authority of the rider. It should have been overcome during initial training on the flat, but you must be continually on the lookout for signs of it. Common manifestations of nappiness in jumping are: refusing to jump, running out, wanting to leave the ring to return to the 'herd' in the collecting ring, and refusing to jump away from the collecting ring. At the slightest indications of nappiness in jumping training, act straight away. Ask yourself these questions:

(1) Is the fence a new and frightening one? If so, show it to the pony; let him rub his nose on it; let him watch a mature pony jump it; let him follow such a pony over it. You should show him a new fence before asking him to jump it. YOUR FAULT.

(2) Is the fence too high for him? If so, lower it to well within his known capacity and try again. You have proceeded too fast. YOUR FAULT.

(3) Is the rider sufficiently competent and confident for a young pony? Is the pupil receiving a jab in the mouth, or is the rider getting left behind? Again – YOUR FAULT.

(4) Do the saddle and bridle fit properly; is the pony comfortable in his mouth? If not, sort it out – YOUR FAULT.

(5) Is he given his head at the right moment so that he can balance himself? If not – YOUR FAULT.

(6) Are you asking him to jump directly into the sun or a bright reflection? A daft thing to do to a novice. YOUR FAULT.

(7) Is he sound? Is he in pain?

You should be satisfied on all these points – after all, you should know; you have trained him so far and know him better than anybody else. However, you must combat this nappiness, (unless the pony is unsound or in pain) before you finish the session. Lower the jump, alter it, swap riders, follow him with a lunge whip, anything reasonable – but you must insist, then reward him. Finish with something easy, on a good note. You have had a minor set-back; try to avoid another.

Rushing

Most ponies enjoy jumping and can get very excited about it. This can become a bad habit very quickly and they jump out of control. You will get very low marks indeed for manners.

If you make jumping training a natural extension of the work on the flat then this is less likely to be a problem; your pony can pop over the odd low jump during a session on the flat; if he gets excited trot him round until he settles before trying again. The same principle applies right through his schooling for jumping; if he gets excited, stop jumping and do something else for a while.

The ultimate aim is to canter round a course of jumps at a

'hunting pace' but if the pony is hotting up during his schooling it will be necessary to bring him back to the trot after every jump and settle him before attempting the next fence. At this point in his training it is only necessary to canter the last few paces.

In the later stages of his training, if he still tends to rush, then a pole on the ground, or better a raised one which he has to pop over in the manner of a bounce fence, is a useful device. He can trot up to this pole, jump it, then his hind feet should be in exactly the right place to take off to jump the fence.

The optimum position of this pole will depend on the size and length of stride of your pony and the type of fence, the take-off for a spread being further away than that for an upright. You will get this exactly right by trial. Watch him jump without the ground pole and notice where his hind feet leave the ground. Put the pole in such a position that when he pops the pole it puts him right into that position. For a 14 hh pony taking a 3 ft 3 ins (1 m) upright fence, you may need to put the pole on the ground 10 ft (3 m) away. He will look at this pole very hard, which will take his mind off rushing the fence. If he stops looking at it and becomes careless, knocking the fence poles, then you have continued this exercise too long. Do something else.

Another way of combating rushing fences is trotting round in circles adjacent to the jump, as shown in Fig. 8.5. If the pony gets excited, trot round until he settles. Then take the jump, return to the circles and re-take the fence only when he and you are ready.

Sorting out the problem of rushing fences is very important

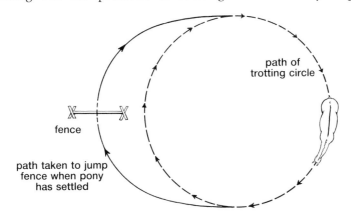

path of
trotting circle

fence

path taken to jump
fence when pony
has settled

Fig. 8.5 Using trot circles to settle the pony who rushes his fences. Retake the jump only when rider and pony are ready.

because if your pony approaches his fence with his head up, straining at the bit, not only will he jump badly, taking off in the wrong place, with a hollow back, and probably knocking a pole, but also your style marks will be low. He must learn to tackle his courses at an even pace, not too slowly nor too fast, on the bit, ready for the rider to regulate the jumping for whatever situation presents itself.

Tearing off after jumping

Sometimes a pony will tear away as soon as he lands, and maybe put in a buck or two; again, this must be nipped in the bud. You will have to forget about cantering round at a good hunting pace for the time being. As soon as he lands make him trot and carry on doing this until he no longer associates jumping with tanking off. Go back a few stages in his training; you may have to bring him to a halt after each jump and reward him with encouraging words and a pat on the neck. The circle-trotting exercise described above is also very useful for this problem, as you can wait for him to settle down before attempting another jump.

Laziness

Older ponies can become a bit lazy; they learn to jump with minimum effort, taking off too close to the jumps, missing the poles narrowly, maybe rattling them all. We call them 'brinksmen' and they have to be reminded to take off in the right spot and extend themselves, otherwise you will soon have a pony perfectly capable of clear rounds, knocking off one or two poles at nearly every show – a very frustrating state of affairs. The pony's re-education at home should consist of very low, wide parallels, like those used in his initial training. These will make the pony stretch. The rider should be encouraged to give stronger leg aids on the take-off.

Refusing and running out

This is one of the greatest problems in jumping, and is often caused by the rider. If the rider is at all half-hearted about jumping a fence, his pony will pick up the signals straight away. The rider must assume the pony is going to jump the fence, then, more than likely, he will, because his positive thoughts have been transmitted to the pony.

However, when a refusal does happen, something has to be done about it. Look back at the paragraphs on nappiness; there are lots of clues there. Basically the jockey should ride more forcefully and try again. If this does not work, attack the fence from a different angle. If unsuccessful, never approach a fence the same way twice; there is simply no point. If all else fails, take the fence down to a lower level so that he can jump it without losing face, and gradually build it up again until it is at the original height. After this, much praise. Running out usually occurs because the rider takes the pony into the fence at an angle, and this gives the pony the opportunity to slip out sideways, sometimes because he could not jump the fence from that position.

Occasionally a pony will refuse for a very good reason, which may be that he has seen something unsafe that you have missed, perhaps barbed wire or a hazard on the landing side. In an honest pony this can be a life-saver for you both.

MORE ADVANCED JUMPING TRAINING

Ditches with or without water

There are many WHPs which stop at ditches but which tackle other jumps with ease. Although this can be due to the rider (a possibility which should not be overlooked) it probably indicates a lack of experience in the pony. Perhaps the best way to teach a pony to tackle this sort of hazard is in the hunting field: he will be so keen not to be left behind that he will jump most things. Ponies love to jump in company, and will fly over fences that they would not jump in cold blood.

However, not everyone has the opportunity to hunt, and anyway it is as well to start the training at home. So dig yourself a ditch, fill it with water if possible, and use it in a variety of ways. You can place a fence either in front of it, behind it, or over it, or leave it as a simple ditch. Jump it in as many ways as possible and in all directions. Use it as part of a combination of two or three fences. A permanent ditch must have poles let into the ground to support the edges. Peg it very carefully so that there are no dangerous projections to trip over.

Water jumps

Some permanent showgrounds have water jumps originally intended for show-jumpers. These are usually shallow concrete trays set into the ground and lined with rubber mats. They are often deeper in the middle and slope to merge with the ground at the take-off and landing sides. There is usually a low fence sloping away on the approach side and a white tape on the landing side. To jump with no faults the pony must clear the tape with all four feet.

A certain speed is necessary to take these water jumps, i.e. an extended canter. However, avoid the mistake of approaching the obstacle at a mad gallop. The pony must be free to extend his neck and adjust in the air, and must not be too tightly held in the mouth.

There is a water jump in the ring at Peterborough which has been used at the championship from time to time. Take every opportunity you can to practise this kind of jump until your pony understands what is required.

Bounce fences

It is not difficult to teach a pony how to cope with a bounce fence. Indeed if he has been trained along the lines we suggest he will have already bounced on the approach to a jump in order to place himself correctly. On the other hand, if he has never done a bounce before, he will be lost when faced with one in the ring.

Bridges

These are no longer recommended for inclusion in BSPS courses. This is disappointing since bridges always sort out the proper hunters from the rest. Certainly, in our part of the world, one has to be able to go over bridges when hunting, or be left behind. However, a badly made bridge in a ring can be very dangerous indeed.

Pens

These are related jumps, enclosed at the sides, sometimes incorporating a change of direction. The exit jump must, however,

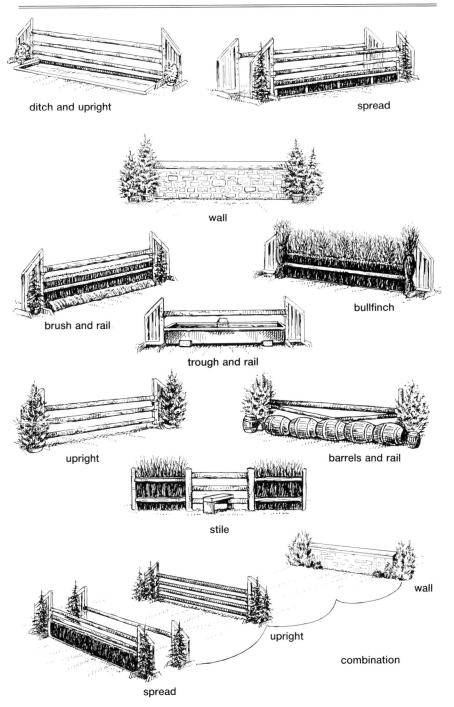

Fig. 8.6 Different types of fence.

be visible on the approach to the entry jump. Make a pen at home with alternative exits. Your pony will need to be collected and listening for your aids; if he does not know which exit you are about to take he will have to concentrate.

Combinations with three or more elements

These need practice because unless you get the approach and bascule right for the first element, by the time you get to the third, you and your pony will be totally unbalanced and in a terrible mess. Practise them at home, going back to basics if necessary.

Jumping into a wood

If a show is positioned in a field next to a covert, it creates a wonderful opportunity for a coursebuilder to test the boldness of the competitors. Siting a jump on the boundary between the two creates another test which 'sorts the men from the boys', and again, hunting seems to offer good training. If your pony has not met this situation before he may be unwilling to co-operate, especially on a sunny day, when he has to jump into a dense, dark woodland.

Over the 'edge of the world'

Undulating showgrounds offer opportunities to test the ponies in various ways. One such test is to put a solid fence right on top of a hill or on the edge of a dip. On approach it looks as if you have to jump into a void. This is another test of boldness.

Consideration of the foregoing goes towards explaining many aspects of the WHP scene: a WHP does not reach his prime sometimes until he is about ten years old. There is a lot to learn.

Some ponies consistently win all summer at the big shows in rings which are as level as a bowling green, offering little opportunity to the coursebuilder. But these ponies often fail at hunt supporters' shows over differing terrain. Nor do they necessarily do well over the more challenging courses at the championships. They have good conformation and manners but lack varied experience and sometimes boldness.

Some children seem to go from one successful pony to another. They are good riders and WHPs do need riding well.

JUMPING THE OLDER PONY

Assuming that your pony is an accomplished and reliable jumper, well mannered at all times, and well schooled on the flat, then you will not need to work him at home day after day, except perhaps at the beginning of the season. In fact, if you do, he will soon get very bored and it will begin to show in the ring. He will need to be kept reasonably fit and offered interest and variety in his life, perhaps through hacking over differing terrain.

With the experienced pony the only jumping you will need to do during the main part of the season is in the collecting ring.

Towards the championships you will want to offer him something more challenging; for many, Pony Club eventing can be the answer. The cross-country phase provides excellent experience for both pony and rider, and it helps to get the pony fit enough for the twenty or so fences he will be required to jump on the big day.

Beckfield Ben Hur – supreme winner in 1968, 1969 and 1972. Small for his class but good enough to win. (Photo: *Clive Hiles*)

GENERAL CONCLUSIONS

Your rider must be every bit as well trained as your pony, or he will spoil all your hard work in one short lesson. If your rider is more experienced than your pony, this is a good state of affairs, and will help to give the pony confidence. The rider must have an independent seat, and tactful hands, and be able to anticipate difficulties so that he can help the pony to put himself right. He must be able to help the pony to shorten or lengthen his stride when necessary, and be able to judge when the pony is so badly placed at a fence that it would be tactful to circle round it instead. This avoids mistakes that can frighten the pony. Taking a pony to an indoor school to jump the first few times is a good idea as the enclosure will help him to concentrate, and stop him from thinking of naughty ideas like tanking off. Only jump out-of-doors when he is sufficiently confident, and you will feel he is ready. If jumping indoors is not possible for you, then limit your training to a confined area in the field.

Be very patient with his training; it is never worth hurrying the process. If you do, you will regret it. Remember to keep the pony interested, and include lots of fun and variety in his work; he must never be allowed to get bored or sour.

Some ponies have more ability than others, and your programme should take this into account. However, the pony with ability will be inclined to be rushed. So beware – take it steady.

One of the best training grounds is the hunting field, so when the pony is progressing well and is confident, he may be taken cub-hunting, and then later on, hunting. A season's hunting is good for both rider and pony, as they will meet all sorts of obstacles and problems. In the company of others, neither will wish to be left behind, so they learn to cope and get themselves out of difficult situations. In so doing they gain confidence in one another, have fun into the bargain, and are more able to do well together in the show ring.

CHAPTER 9

Tack and Clothing

TACK

There are certain types of bridles and saddles that are most suitable for hunter ponies. Basically, a SHP should wear a simple double bridle with a plain front (browband) and noseband. His saddle should be a straight-cut show saddle, preferably with a slight knee roll for the rider's comfort.

A WHP should wear a simple snaffle or double bridle, again with a plain front and noseband. His saddle should be discreetly cut to show off his shoulder, but giving jumping security for the jockey by having knee and thigh rolls.

Gadgets have no place in a well-schooled pony's wardrobe. Dropped nosebands, martingales, breastplates, and severe bits will all tell the judge that the pony might misbehave, or that the jockey cannot cope.

There are several aspects to consider when buying saddlery; comfort of pony and jockey, effectiveness, colour, quality and size. Look at the picture as a whole and try to choose tack which is quiet in colour and unobtrusive in style. If you are buying secondhand items they are more likely to be of a mellow colour and to match.

If you need a new saddle, buy it in the autumn, then you will have the winter to ride it in and gradually mellow it in time for the showing season. If any stuffing is needed this can be done by your saddler before the season starts.

The regular winter cleaning will help the leather to acquire a good deep colour. Avoid pale-coloured saddles as these rarely take on the desired hue. If your new saddle is not dark enough ask your saddler to stain it, or put some neatsfoot oil on the rough side of the leather.

Before using a new saddle, we oil it several times on the rough side, i.e., the suede or flesh side, and massage saddle soap into the smooth grain side. This helps supple it and makes it waterproof, avoiding rain marks.

New bridles are taken apart and each strap soaked individually in a tin of neatsfoot oil, then rubbed dry with a soft cloth for a few minutes. We have found this treatment ensures a good colour and a waterproof start to a long supple life.

What to buy

If you have bought a made pony, be guided by the saddle and bridle he is used to. If he goes well in a particular bit or bridle, there is no point in changing it. However, if you have a young pony which you are having to make, choose the kindest bit that will achieve the results you want.

Start off with a simple snaffle bridle and take the pony out for a ride in an enclosed area where he can be easily controlled. If, for instance, his usual tack includes a dropped noseband and running martingale, or something more severe, watch him carefully when he is ridden, and decide whether he really needs them.

If you consider he does not, first change his noseband to a plain cavesson, and if all goes well and he is responding kindly, in due course, take off the running martingale. If having removed

Fig. 9.1 Untidy rider and pony. Note sloppy turn-out, use of gadgets and unsuitable tack.

these items you find the pony is not going well, you will have to reinstate them; perhaps at a later date, when schooling has improved him, you may be able to try the exercise again. Extra gadgets spoil the looks of a working pony in the show ring, and it is better to do without them if at all possible.

To create a good overall picture, the saddle and bridle should match each other in colour and quality. The bridle should be the right weight of leather for the pony's head, and the reins the correct length, i.e. when the pony is standing, with the jockey on board holding the reins, there should not be more than 10 ins (25 cm) to spare on the double.

The bridle

The bridle for a hunter pony head wants to be less dainty than for a show pony. Be critical about the width of the straps and reins, and be sure that they are in proportion to the pony. If your pony is finer than you would wish, consider different proportions and styles to achieve a more workmanlike result. For example, a dainty Thoroughbred type might benefit from wearing a snaffle bridle with a running martingale.

Most people know how to fit a bridle, but the most common mistake is to fasten the throatlash too tightly. Remember that

Fig. 9.2 Beautifully turned out combination wearing correct dress and simple tack.

when the pony flexes his head and neck, he will require more room under his throat, or his breathing may be restricted.

The weight of the curb chain needs to be in proportion to the bit. It is essential to stop a pelham or curb bit from turning forwards in the pony's mouth, and provides leverage on the lower jaw to encourage flexing at the poll.

The reins

The reins should be neat. If there are two reins, then the top one can be a laced one to give extra purchase on a wet day. Rubber reins look a bit bright, but if they give a child more confidence, it is better to use them; change to a neater rein when the jockey becomes more accomplished. On a pelham or double bridle the wider rein goes on the bridoon, or top bit, and the narrower one goes on the curb bit. To be correct, the curb reins should be joined together with a buckle fastening, but the bridoon reins should be stitched together. If a running martingale is used it should go on the curb rein, using rubber rein stops to avoid the ring getting caught on the bit.

There are always arguments about which rein the martingale should go on, but since the snaffle rein asks the pony to raise his head, it would seem illogical to attach to it a device that would pull it down. Remember, the snaffle rein raises the head, and the curb rein asks the pony to flex at the poll, relax the jaw and bring his head down, so do not work against this principle.

Bits

When choosing a bit, having decided which type the pony goes best in, select one which is neat without being severe. Very thin bits can be too sharp for the mouth and can be cruel. Preferably use the same colour metal for the bit and stirrup irons. If a thick mouthpiece is preferred, check by looking in the side of the pony's mouth that there is room for the bit when his mouth is closed. If not, the pony will be uncomfortable, and the bars of the mouth will become bruised.

Do not forget the lip strap. This little strap is attached to the side of the curb bit, goes through the fly link on the curb chain, and therefore stops the curb chain from being lost if it becomes undone.

Some ponies prefer certain metal for their bits, and will go more sweetly in one than with another. This may be something to do with the acidity of the saliva. So bear this in mind. The pony must accept the bit; signs of an accepted bit are; a closed mouth, that is wet, even foamy, with a relaxed jaw. Indications of discomfort are an open mouth leading to dryness, and general resistance such as jaw crossing and pulling at the rider's hands.

As with all saddlery, there is an element of fashion even in bitting – at one time show hacks were regularly ridden in Kimblewicks!

There are so many bits to choose from, that it is worth looking in a textbook to see all the types and how they work. The jointed snaffle is generally believed to be a mild bit, but some ponies find the nutcracker action too severe. If this is so, try a French snaffle, which has two joints in the mouth. This helps the bit to curve around the mouth comfortably. Another good bit to try is the short-cheeked pelham, either jointed or straight. It is a mild bit and makes a good transition from the snaffle to the double bridle. Severe bits have no place in the show ring, and any pony that needs such a bit should be taken home and schooled with care and consideration. A hunter pony needs to be well behaved and balanced to do well, so any resistances incurred from incorrect bitting will surely put him down the line.

The bit in a pony's mouth is one of the links for conversation between pony and rider, so not only consider the bit and its fitting, but also the hands of the rider, and whether or not they are sympathetic.

Gadgets

Dropped nosebands and martingales are sometimes necessary, but do try to dispense with them as soon as possible. Some judges will penalise their use, certainly if equality of marks requires another look. However, it is paramount that a child feels safe and that the pony goes calmly, so use them until both can happily go without.

The dropped noseband stops the pony from crossing his jaw and from opening his mouth. These are both resistances; the fault may lie in the rider's hands, so with training, both must learn to give and take.

The running martingale helps to keep a pony straight into

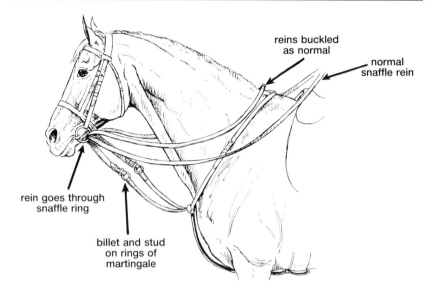

Fig. 9.3 Method of attaching running reins which allows for the running rein to be dropped when not needed and picked up only when required.

his fences and provides a handy neck strap if the rider needs it. However, it must be fitted so that it does not interfere with the direct line between bit and hand on the rein. Only when the pony's head is raised above the desired level will the rein become 'bent'. Originally two reins were used on a snaffle bit; this was to ensure that the martingale was only used when needed; the martingale was threaded on to only one rein, leaving the other free to use when the martingale was not required. This was a sensible arrangement which avoided interfering with the pony's mouth.

If head throwing is a major problem, the standing martingale is the more appropriate choice because the pony is less likely to suffer a jab in his mouth. It will restrain him, and perhaps stop the habit. If a running martingale is used for this purpose, the pony will soon learn that he can throw his head up as well as snatch the reins away from the rider's hands. However, the standing variety will soon show that there are limits to head tossing.

Be patient: time and care will solve most of your problems. You will see many gadgets at a show, particularly a show-jumping one. Have a good look at them. Running reins and side reins should only be used in the most gentle way. They can certainly be very cruel, and develop muscles in all the wrong places. One of the kindest running reins to use, if one is needed, is as follows: use two pairs of reins and a snaffle bit, along with a running martingale. Use one pair of reins as usual, attached to the bit; attach the bit ends of the other pair to the rings of the martingale, then thread the reins through the snaffle rings of the bit, and then buckle them on top of the neck. When used like this, the running rein can be dropped when not needed, and picked up only when required. (See Fig. 9.3.)

The saddle

Your saddle needs to be a simple affair without extra embellishments. A jumping saddle with large knee rolls and a high seat is not appropriate. However, a straight-cut show saddle offers no support to an active jumping competitor, so something in between must be sought. A small knee roll is suitable; also a straight cut-back head (pommel) is useful as this type of saddle fits most ponies over the withers. Be sure there is enough width across the waist of the saddle because this is needed to take the rider's thigh in comfort. Apart from fitting the pony well and being the right size for the jockey, make sure the saddle looks right and is discreet. Some saddles do have curious proportions.

Girths

A girth to complement the saddle would be a show girth made out of leather. This is particularly suitable for smaller ponies. Larger ponies need a stronger girth, so we suggest a good Atherstone. Be careful in your choice here because there are cheap versions on the market, and they can be recognised by the wrinkling of the leather. If you prefer another kind of girth look around the shows and choose one to suit you, but be sure it is strong and not cumbersome.

Stirrups and leathers

Remember that children grow, and check occasionally that the leathers are the correct length. If they become worn in one place, have the buckles moved. Stirrup irons need to be ½ in. (12.5 mm) wider (inside) than the width of the jockey's boot, so that the foot will come out in case of an accident. However, a large stirrup can be dangerous as the foot could go right through the iron. The Peacock, or safety iron, is very suitable for any pony in classes up to 14 hh; this has a strong rubber band on the outside which comes off in an emergency. If at all possible do choose stainless steel for irons because it is strong. Nickel iron can crush the foot if banged hard.

Always choose the best quality tack you can afford. You will always be happier with it, it will last longer, be safer, and keep its value.

CLOTHES FOR THE PONY

The pony that is stabled or travelling will need rugs and bandages. If he is clipped he will need at least two blankets under his rug and possibly a cotton sheet next to his skin to keep him and the rugs clean. This is easily washed.

Do not do up the front of his rugs too tightly as he needs to stretch his neck to eat and drink. Bandages may be necessary if his legs have been clipped, but intuition will tell you if he is warm enough without. He will certainly need them if his legs have just been washed.

New Zealand rugs are only needed if the weather is very cold or wet, or if the pony is clipped and you wish to put him out for a few hours. Use your discretion. If it is cold but dry, and he looks well and is fed well he may well do better without one. Once a rug has been worn, the coat becomes flattened and does not do its job of keeping the pony warm because the insulating pockets of air have been squashed out. However if you are at all worried, use one, and do not take it off until the weather is warmer again.

Certainly once it has rained continuously for twelve hours, you must bring the pony inside and get him dry and warm; and this may be the time to make a decision about the wearing of a New Zealand rug.

Basically these rugs have a chest strap, possibly a girth, and leg straps for the hind legs. Do not do up the chest strap too tightly, nor the girth, just have them tight enough to be comfortable and to stay in place. The best, self-righting New Zealand rugs do not have girths. The leg straps are usually crossed over each other and fastened on the same side from whence they came.

If the weather is really cold, or your pony is clipped, you can successfully put on an old rug underneath his New Zealand. He will be far healthier going out like this than staying in his box all day. Spending twenty-four hours in a box is exceedingly boring and can encourage stable vices.

There is a tremendous choice of stable rugs on the market, so if you buy one choose a lightweight one that can be easily washed. It is hard work rugging up a pony with old-fashioned heavy rugs; also they are tiring for the pony. Use thick foam under the roller to avoid pressure on the spine, and try to use an arched roller. You can also put a piece of foam over the wither to prevent sores.

Stable bandages are usually made of a warm material and are put over gamgee tissue, soft cotton material, or thin foam. They are put on from just under the knee, and go right down to the top of the hoof. They are used to keep him warm or clean. The modern way to travel is to use stable bandages and put leg protectors over the top. However, if the weather is very hot, the protectors can be used alone, but never be tempted to travel without any protection. Leg protectors usually cover both the knees and the hocks, and go right down to the ground. They are easily put on with Velcro fastenings. If you decide to use some sort of protection for the legs when jumping at home the easiest boots to put on are those with strong Velcro fastenings, the best ones are made of leather. There are many styles of over-reach boots, tendon boots, and speedy-cutting boots to choose from.

CLOTHES FOR THE RIDER

Riding a pony in a WHP class is an athletic sport so it is important that the jockey's clothes are comfortable. Taking trouble with the details of your rider's clothes could win you an extra place in the ring, simply because the well-dressed jockey looks neater and more professional than a less carefully dressed child.

The jodhpurs need to be a quiet colour, finishing neatly at the ankle where they fit over a good pair of jodhpur boots. Elastic may be fitted to go under the instep to keep everything in place. If breeches are worn (these are suitable for the 15 hh classes) the rider needs a good pair of rubber or leather top boots which have garter straps at the top. Originally garter straps were worn threaded between the buttons at the bottom of the breeches, and this helped to keep the boots in place at the tops. Buy the best boots you can afford.

Sandman – supreme winner at Peterborough in 1986, owned by Mr L. Connor. This pony is wearing a double bridle and his jockey has long boots, suitable for an older rider.

A well-fitting jacket made of tweed, plain navy or black fabric should be cut long enough to touch the cantle of the saddle at the back. A jacket with a waist seam fits better than one without. If the collar is made of velvet, try to match the jockey's cap to this. The cap must be a safe one: your child's safety is more important than looks, although these caps need not look ugly. There are now new rules about the wearing of safety headgear, so make sure you are aware of these. Certainly during the jumping phase an approved cap with a chin-strap should be worn. During the showing phase, when a showing hat is worn, a girl wears the elastic behind the head under the hair, and this looks very nice; however, a boy looks more appropriately dressed with the elastic under the chin.

A shirt may be any quiet colour so long as it blends with the general scheme chosen. The collar needs to be well cut to stay in place. Choose a tie that goes with everything else and tie it neatly.

Gloves should be brown, as should the whip or cane. Button-

Randall's Sovereign. A happy picture of Mrs Gunn's beautifully turned-out pony and smiling child rider. Note the foot elastic sewn on to the jodhpurs.
(Photo: Ray Kennedy)

holes are not worn.

Thought and care in dressing girls' hair will be well rewarded. Look at other children to find ideas of styles. Use a hairnet to keep it tidy. Short hair is the most difficult because it is inclined to stick out, so use hair spray and grips. Long hair is easier to manage and can be plaited or pinned into a neat bun at the nape of the neck. Boys need to have their hair cut short unless they are prepared to wear a hairnet too!

If hair ribbons are used, again choose a discreet colour. Remember to round off the corners of the back number card and to tie it round the waist with a piece of narrow elastic or velvet ribbon. Tuck the knot away inside the front of the jacket by passing it through a buttonhole, and check that the number is the right way up. If you are entered in several classes, it is wise to make notes on the back of each number so there is no confusion on the day as to which number is needed for which pony and for which class.

CHAPTER 10

Transport

It is important that your pony arrives at the show as fresh as possible. Travelling can be quite a stressful business, so careful consideration must be given to the pony's requirements and those of the people accompanying him. When travelling, the pony may be subjected to physical stresses from a variety of sources, e.g. vibration (which must cause wear on joints); excessive noise, and bad driving, especially cornering and sudden braking, particularly downhill. Mental tension may be suffered through being bullied by other ponies, through an inability to see what is going on around him and even through the company of anxious and therefore irritable humans.

Ponies must not be allowed to bully each other when boxed. They should be on a rope short enough to prevent this. However, ponies do need some freedom of movement and must be able to hold their heads in a natural position. Some central partitions are extended at the front to overcome the problem.

All partitions should go down to the floor. If the gap at the bottom is 2 ins (5 cm) or more, feet will go under and there is a risk of damaging the coronet band. If a partition is more than about 12 ins (30 cm) from the floor, adjacent horses can tread on each other's feet, again risking injury. It is quite useful to have the bottom 18 ins (45 cm) or so made of heavy rubber, which gives protection to the lower legs and allows for easy cleaning out.

You must make sure that the pony has room to spread his legs to balance himself, and that the floor is of the non-slip variety.

There should be no space between the ramp and the body of the box or trailer. This is something to watch out for if you use a cattle truck. It has been known for a foal's leg to slip through such a gap.

A wooden base with hardwood bars bolted on to it crossways provides a good surface for a ramp. Carriage bolts which pass right through the bars and the ramp, with nuts and washers on the outside, are best. Wood screws or nails are simply not up to the job and should not be used. If the ramp is covered with any other material, it is important that it does not get slippery, especially when wet, when it wears, or when very dry. All horses and ponies travel better with a broad breast bar at the correct height and a breech strap behind. If you travel 12.2 hh ponies in a box designed for 16 handers the breast bar will press on the ponies' windpipe. Interior padding makes for extra comfort but it is essential that there are no protrusions, especially metal fittings, at knee or hock level.

Floors are usually wooden, double thickness with laths bolted on in strategic positions to help the ponies grip and keep their balance. Drain holes should be sited in suitable positions, to allow urine to seep away.

The type of transport you select will depend on many factors including the length of journeys to be undertaken, the type and surface of the roads, the frequency of travelling, the finance available and amount of parking space at home. The further and more frequently you travel, the more necessary it becomes to have expensive transport. Those who take part in the major shows up and down the country, couldn't contemplate using a trailer, and many have vehicles built on a bus chassis to give the best possible ride for their animals.

We presently use a three-ton Bedford TK specially adapted for our needs. It is fitted to take two ponies at the back, one facing forward and the other backwards, with the space at the front converted for family use. There is a groom's walkway between the two animals, so we can plait up on route.

TRAILERS

If you restrict your showing to one or two hours' travelling each way a trailer will probably be adequate. One problem with trailers is that they tend to rattle, which is very noisy for the passengers.

When buying one it can be very revealing to take a short ride in the trailer yourself (not on the road, as we understand to do so is illegal). Trailers come in many different designs. Some have two wheels whilst others have four wheels on two axles. We have found the latter easier to reverse and more stable on the road. Also, they stand without tipping when disconnected from the towing vehicle.

Range Rovers or long-wheelbase Land Rovers make good towing vehicles, and off the road, having four-wheel drive is an obvious advantage. The tow ball should be fitted to the vehicle so that the trailer is level and the ponies must be positioned correctly within the trailer so that it is balanced with neither too much nor too little of their weight being carried on the ball. The breast bar and breech strap will control their position to ensure this.

We have a double trailer which has just one ramp, at the rear. Our ponies soon learn to exit backwards; and to facilitate this a low-slung trailer having a ramp with a shallow incline is much the best. An open front ramp does encourage a reluctant loader to enter the trailer but if you don't have a front ramp a window at the front will help to entice the pony in and enable him to see out while travelling, which may help him settle. A groom's door giving access to the front of the trailer is essential.

Breech straps are desirable to prevent ponies rushing out backwards as soon as the ramp is put down but the height of breech straps is very important. If they are designed for a horse then they may be too high for a pony.

If the central partition is hinged at the front, the rear end can be pushed to one side to entice a shy loader; and if the partition is totally removable then the trailer can also be more usefully employed for other tasks, such as moving bales of hay and straw.

Wooden floors can rot so always muck out as soon as you get home to allow the boards to dry off. Trailers are durable, so a growing family with ponies of increasing size might as well buy one big enough to last. Ours is 7 ft 2 ins (2.6 m) high, floor to roof, and takes two 15 hh ponies happily. Our trailer was made to our specification eighteen years ago and it still has life in it yet.

MAINTENANCE

Horseboxes will only last if they are properly maintained. The brakes will require regular professional attention and the tyres and lights must be checked frequently.

Attention with an oil can and rag is rewarding: fasteners will be easier to use, and hinges on ramps will run smoother. Always wipe off excess oil to protect your clothes.

Most suspensions, tow mechanisms and other moving parts will need lubrication for a smooth ride and long life. Tightening loose nuts reduces rattling.

CARE OF PONIES IN TRANSIT

The amount of rugging your pony should wear for travelling will depend on the weather, but leg protection is absolutely necessary at all times. You can use either all-in-one snap-on leg protectors, or bandages plus knee and hock pads. The all-in-one leg protectors are expensive but convenient to use and offer maximum protection. A tail bandage should be worn, and for a pony who rubs his tail it may be necessary to fit a tail guard as well, which can be attached to the roller on the rug.

Some horses need a poll pad in case they hit their heads on the roof, but ponies are smaller and unlikely to need one. The headcollar should be sturdy and, as always, the lead rope should be tied to a loop of binder twine on a tie-ring to avoid damage to the headcollar if the pony runs back.

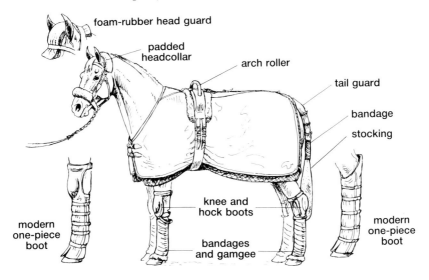

Fig. 10.1 Correct dress for travelling. Use lighter or heavier rugs depending on the time of year.

If the pony is difficult to load spend time at home practising the drill. It may be helpful to feed the pony in the trailer or box every feed time, every day, until he goes in without hesitation. He can then be taken out for short trips and praised when he settles well.

Always drive especially slowly for the first ten minutes of a journey to give the ponies time to settle down and to arrange their limbs for comfort and balance.

Go round corners very carefully and slowly. This extra care will give confidence to the ponies – a bad traveller can make showing a misery.

Obvious symptoms of stress are shivering and trembling, but these can also indicate extreme tiredness. Bear in mind that a pony always loses weight when travelling, and he will lose a great deal more if he is uncomfortable, under stress, or arrives home very tired. It is a good idea to allow the pony to have a complete day off after a day out at a show.

CHAPTER 11

The Show

THE DAY BEFORE

If you have to make an early start on the day of the show, your pony will need to be prepared the day before. If he is stable kept he will need only an extra grooming, but if grass kept he will need shampooing. Don't allow him to catch cold – if necessary wash a small area at a time and dry it before continuing.

We suggest that you begin with the head, neck and mane and then dry these. Then wash the shoulder and forelegs. Next will be the back, loins, quarters and hind legs, followed by the tail. Be sure he is dry and warm and rug him up well. Put on a tail bandage, possibly first having put the tail into a stocking to keep it clean. Put large pieces of foam or wadding on to his lower legs and bandage these in place to keep him warm and clean. Leave plaiting until either late evening or early morning; if in doubt about the plaits getting rubbed, you will have to get up especially early to do the job before you go.

If there is anything vital you must remember before you depart, leave yourself a note in a special place so that you see it in the morning.

Load up your transport the evening before, except perhaps for the food and coffee; but do as much as you can beforehand so that you have very little to do in the morning.

SHOW CHECK-LIST

The following is a list of equipment that you may need for attending a show, plus a few chores to carry out before you set off. You won't need to take everything on the list but it will help serve as a reminder.

Transport

Hay-nets
Short feed
Bedding

Water carrier
Water bucket

Driver

Map
Entry tickets
Check tyres, oil and water
Oil any rattling parts
Money

Show entry lorry stickers
Fill up petrol or diesel
Check safety of vehicle
Tachograph papers
    (if appropriate)

Tack

Exercise saddle
Show saddles
Girths
Whips

Exercise bridle
Show bridles
Stirrup irons and leathers
Spare headcollar

First aid

FOR PEOPLE
TCP
Scissors
Lint
Plasters
Disprin
Elastic bandages
Cotton wool
Any special medication

FOR PONIES
Antiseptic powder
Hoof pick
Leg wash
Gamgee tissue
Leg bandages
Tail bandage
Vick
Liniment*
Antiseptic spray
Poultice

(*If your pony hits a pole or fence while jumping in the ring it is a good idea to sponge the leg well with one part liniment to four parts water, cover with gamgee or foam and bandage. This could save bruising being a prolonged problem, and should be done as soon as possible after the incident.)

Vanity box

Hair ribbons
Hair brush and comb
Scissors
Safety pins
Hairnets
Small sewing kit
Elastic bands

Clothes brush
Waist elastic or ribbon
Hair grips and pins
Schedule
Exhibitor's number
Vaccination certificates
Membership cards

Plaiting box

Blunt plaiting needle
Elastic bands
Scissors
Mane comb

Comb for squares on
    quarters
Black, white or brown
    button thread

Grooming box

Body brush
Water brush
Hoof oil and brush
Hoof pick
Rubber curry comb
Saddle soap and sponge
Vaseline
Fly repellent

Dandy brush
2 rubbers
Hoof oil
Whitening if needed
2 sponges
Baby oil
Vick
2 towels

Fig. 11.1 Tack box and contents.

Extras for the ring

Best body brush
Bucket and small amount
  of water

Small rubber or towel
Sponge
Hoof oil and brush

The pony

Travelling blankets
Waterproof rug for ring
Leg bandages
Knee pads
Hock boots
Tail stocking
Lunge line

Travelling rugs
Show blanket for ring
Bandage pads or gamgee
Snap-on leg protectors
Tail bandages
Headcollar and rope
Cavesson

The rider

Exercise hat
Jodhpurs
Shirt and tie
Gloves
Breeches
Anoraks
Waterproof boots
Spare trousers

Best hat
Jacket
Jodhpur boots
Long black boots
Waistcoat for cold weather
Over-trousers
Warm jersey

It is a good idea to photo-copy your entries, including the cheque on the copy. It can happen that you arrive at a show and find that the secretary has not received your entry, so proof that you have sent it is most important. Take the photo-copy with you, along with lorry pass, back numbers, and any tickets you may need.

ON ARRIVAL

Depending on the size of the show and the time needed to warm up your pony, you should arrive on the ground at least one hour before your first class. On arrival each team member should know what to do: fetch the number from the secretary; find out whether the show is running on time, etc. Park your lorry so that it casts shade if it is a hot day, then unload your pony, tie him up to the lorry and remove his travelling gear.

RIDING-IN

Put on your pony's exercise bridle and saddle and send the jockey and pony off to look over the ground, find the ring and generally locate all the facilities which may be needed. Then attend to the serious business of riding the pony in until you are satisfied he is going as you wish; perhaps pop him over an exercise fence a few times.

At all costs avoid getting flustered. Leave enough time to dress the pony and rider in their show clothes and tack.

IN THE RING: THE JUMPING PHASE

The pony and jockey should arrive at the collecting ring in good time, and if competing in a WHP class, the rider should walk the course; this is time well spent. Avoid being the first to jump:

Something Original – supreme winner in 1988, owned by Mr and Mrs Atkinson. His toes are tucked up, he is interested and enjoying himself.
(Photo: *E. L. Gibbs*)

there may be a bogey fence which should be considered carefully beforehand. On entry into the ring the rider should trot purposefully towards the judge, say good morning or good afternoon and tell the steward his/her number. It is not advisable to spend too long riding round the fences: one circle is enough; then get on with the jumping. When the pair have finished their round they should go straight back to the judge, halt and salute. It is rude to leave the ring without this courtesy and to do so could cost you manners marks.

During the jumping phase the best pace is a rhythmic on-going canter, which will provide the necessary impulsion to jump the fences evenly and cleanly. The jockey should try not to slow down after each fence and then speed up for the next, for two reasons. Firstly, it looks untidy; and secondly, a pony is more likely to lose his concentration and balance. However, if a hazard, or an exceptionally tricky fence, is included in the course a decision will have to be made as to what speed is best for this particular problem, but keep to a good rhythm before and after it. Tactics such as these can be decided when walking the course. Smoothness in transitions (or changes of pace) is one of the most difficult things to achieve in the show ring. Many ponies and riders give the impression of falling into the transition, out of control and unbalanced. This is particularly the case in jumping when the speed of the canter keeps changing. Each time a pony increases or decreases his speed at the canter he has an opportunity to resist by altering the position of his head, hollowing his back, losing concentration, trying to go faster than his jockey intends, or to go more slowly, with the possibility of loss of impulsion, resulting in a refusal at a fence. So aim for a pace which suits the pony with the jockey in full control for a particular course.

IN THE RING: THE SHOWING PHASE

On entering the ring the rider should find a space between ponies which are a different colour from his own. The jockey should listen carefully to the steward who will ask the class to walk, trot and canter on one or two reins and then call the ponies into line before giving individual shows.

During the individual show it is important to get each pace just right, paying particular attention to the transitions. The transition should be so smooth and imperceptible that a spectator will realise it has happened but hardly notice at which point it actually took place. The pony's walk should cover a lot of ground with each stride without appearing to hurry. In fact, his walk will reveal a lot about his training and conformation. For example, he will most likely walk well if his quarters are strong and his hind legs are actively engaged, well underneath him. If his shoulder is well laid back, as it should be, he will be able to stride out well with his front legs and carry his head in a comfortable position.

At the trot a pony usually raises his head and shortens the whole length of his body from nose to buttock, therefore, it is logical to anticipate this by shortening the reins at the appropriate moment. The trot should not be fast, nor slow like that of a show hack, but it must remain rhythmic and in true two-time, and in two tracks only. It is no coincidence that this is the pace at which the vet or judge will be most likely to notice any lameness or unevenness. The precise diagonal two-time allows any unevenness to be seen or heard.

The canter needs a slightly longer rein for the pony to stretch his neck and should be mannerly. During the figure-of-eight he must be sufficiently controlled to be obedient to the downward transition through the change of leg, as well as to the upward transition through to the following gallop. It is useful especially for a novice and inexperienced pony or rider, to trot the complete figure-of-eight prior to the canter figure-of-eight, making the movement in two well-defined circles. This helps to settle the pony into his show and gives the jockey time to be sure of the geography of his performance, relative to the show ring and its contents.

The pony should be asked to canter on the correct leg as he goes away from the other ponies, not towards them. This helps him to concentrate. After each canter circle, he should be slowed down and given plenty of room and time to balance himself before being asked to change leg and direction.

The pony must learn to stand still when required, so if he is naughty about this in the ring the jockey could ask the judge if he would allow the rider a moment to quietly insist on a good halt.

Although your rider will have practised the show at home he must be prepared to change its pattern on the day without losing his cool. He should listen carefully to any instructions a steward or judge may give because sometimes a judge may ask for a specific show. If this is the case and your jockey is not aware of

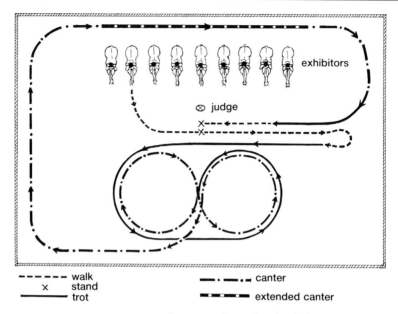

exhibitors

⊗ judge

----- walk
  x   stand
───── trot

—·—·— canter

■—■—■ extended canter

Fig. 11.2 Suggested pattern for individual show.

the judge's wishes, your rider will annoy the judge and lose marks. Sometimes the first few riders do incomplete shows, not because the judge has asked them for something different, but because they are incompetent. In this case, the rider should check with the judge or steward before commencing his usual show.

The basis of a good show is as follows: the pony should be brought out of the line-up for the judge to see, and stood still and square. The rider should be sure that the steward has noted his number. When the judge has looked at the pony he will ask the rider to proceed to show him the pony's paces. The rider should walk directly away from the judge for about twenty yards, turn carefully and trot back, passing the judge in a straight line, before trotting into the figure-of-eight. At this stage a judge can see if the pony moves straight.

If the pony is a novice the circles should not be made too small as he will not be balanced and supple enough for tight turns, but if he is mature he should be able to do neater circles. Smaller circles help to keep the pony's concentration and make the whole show look more professional. If there is time, the jockey can trot a whole figure-of-eight before cantering, making ample preparation for the transitions and change of leg at the centre of the 'eight'. The pair can then extend out of the figure-of-eight and gallop on round the back of the ring, slowing down in good time. They should halt and rein-back a good distance from the judge, then walk forward to a second halt and salute. (If the pony cannot rein-back, he should not be asked to do it.) A judge can see an exhibit better at a distance than one that crowds in on him.

The rider should try to look happy throughout the performance, which will remove some of the tension and could indirectly gain the pair some extra marks. Riders should never chatter to one another in the ring; this is bad manners.

IN THE RING: THE IN-HAND PHASE

After the individual shows, the judge may ask to see the ponies stripped, so the rider should indicate to your groom that he needs him. The rider should stand in front of the pony, facing his head, with one hand either side of the mouth. The groom should take off the saddle and remove any sweat marks.

When it is your rider's turn, he should bring the pony out of line and stand him up squarely in front of the judge, but not too near him. When the judge has looked him over, the pony should be walked away from him, turned and trotted back past the judge, then returned to the line-up. The saddle can now be replaced and the rider can get back on board.

IMPROVING PERFORMANCE

If you are trying to perfect your pony's show, you might find it useful to go to an important show and spend time carefully watching children showing their ponies. Pick out those you feel are really outstanding and try to work out why their shows are so much better than the others. You will probably assume it is because they have the best ponies, but this is often far from the truth. The facts are that they have done their homework and have produced their pony to the highest possible standards. Attention to detail really pays off. In a winning combination the pony looks well and happy, is in good condition and is beautifully trimmed. His saddlery fits neatly and suits him. The jockey is very tidily dressed, and everything is clean and well looked after. The pony's training has been given careful thought and plenty of practice so the whole picture is a pleasure to the eye. Such a pony and jockey make the whole thing look easy. The pony may well have conformation faults and problems but his producers have managed to make the most of his good points. There will always be good ponies in the line-up but they are often put down because they are not properly turned out, or are ridden slovenly, or go round the ring with their ears back.

If you have difficulty with your pony's head carriage, particularly with his putting his head up or poking forward, the simple gadget described on page 138-9 may help. This avoids buying new-fangled draw reins. If used with tact and practice these extra reins encourage a good head carriage and can be dropped or used at will – though certainly not in the show ring.

Galloping can be a problem for some, and too much of it is not good for your pony if the ground is hard. All the judge wants to see is whether the pony can ease himself obediently from a canter to a gallop, showing a real lengthening of stride. A judge does not want to be entertained to a sudden explosion from the canter, followed by a feverish helter-skelter round the ring. The upward transition should show increase of stride and pace into an on-going but controlled gallop, which does not need to be longer than one side of the ring. So go round corners steadily, extend along the straight, and come back into a controlled and balanced canter before the next corner.

The halt and rein-back are not easy movements, and seem to catch out many a rider. They must be practised and perfected at home, as described in Chapter 7.

When faced with a sloping ring your jockey must ask the pony to change legs in the canter uphill. If he tries to change legs on a downward slope, the pony will be unbalanced and find the transition difficult.

Also, if in a ring with a slope, the pony should be made to stand across the lie of the slope, otherwise his conformation may look strange and his framework will not be shown to its best advantage.

When walking the course the rider should use this time to full advantage. He should walk in the tracks he will be taking when riding, and try to judge how the strides between the jumps will be affected by the terrain of the ground. If the going is downhill, the pony will lengthen his stride, and the opposite is true. He should attempt to work out where the tight turns are, and how to use the

The end of a perfect day? Just Jasper, WHP champion of 1984, owned by Mrs C. King. (Photo: Neil B. Jones)

area to best advantage. It is sensible to watch other competitors going round the course, paying special attention to any bogey fences which perhaps were not expected. Try to learn from other people's mistakes; and never be too proud to ask for help.

COURTESY AND SPORTSMANSHIP

Some of the things that mar show days are displays of temper, bad manners, discourtesy, and lack of sportsmanship. Sometimes tension is unbearable, but if your team is to enjoy its day out together, its members must learn to control themselves when under stress. A kind word or a sympathetic approach will help to relax them.

Manners must extend to your attitude to the judge. It is unkind and unfair to find fault with a judge from the ringside; nor should remarks be made in this vein. No one knows, except the judge, what his task is like that day, and many times he will be as disappointed as you that a certain pony he liked did not win, owing perhaps to a jumping fault or lack of manners in its show.

CHAPTER 12

Judging

JUDGING WHP CLASSES

There are several ways a WHP class can be judged, but much will depend on the schedule. A straightforward one will have three classes judged by one judge. In this case, the judge can see the standard of ponies as they jump the course of fences and this is a great help in deciding how to pitch the conformation marks in phase two.

If it is a country show with a strong following of Pony Club and other non-BSPS members, the judge may have a fair assortment of ponies before him. There may be very few ponies worthy of high conformation marks. However, faced with the same schedule at a county show, ponies may be of a very high standard indeed, with only a few marks separating the best ponies. A tactful judge will be more tolerant and generous with his marks at a show of the first description, but the second will tax his ability, and he can afford to be more rigorous to find the rightful winner.

If two judges are appointed for these classes there is often an unexpected result for both judges. It can and must be appreciated that when two judges sort out a class, the result is a compromise unless they both work in a very similar way. Two people can easily prefer two different ponies and hope they win, but there is only one red rosette.

Where one judge has to operate singlehanded, he may bring the ponies back after the jumping phase and place them either in order of their first phase, or he may judge the second phase as a separate show class. Both methods have their drawbacks. If the best jumping-round pony is brought in first, he may well go down after the conformation phase, and this will be very disappointing. If the highest placed conformation pony is brought in first, and then the others brought in order, there is bound to be some sorting out when the marks are added up. However, if it is done this way, the jockeys know roughly how they got on in the jumping phase, and will not necessarily expect to stay in the same places.

At the end of the class it always looks fair if the ponies are lined up in the show order, then, as the final result is calculated, the winners are brought forward, maybe in quite a different order.

JUDGING SHP CLASSES

There are judged as other show classes are judged, but it is advisable to use some sort of marking system, even if it is only a few notes. One needs to be quite sure that a badly behaved pony is not forgotten; also, that very similar ponies are not mixed up. A show hunter pony class can be likened to an adult hunter class except that the judge cannot ride them. The ponies should be unblemished and preferably exhibit a certain amount of presence. Neither of these two characteristics is so important in a WHP class. The approximate apportionment of marks could be: 25% for type and general impression; 25% conformation; 25% straightness of action and freedom of movement; 25% show and manners.

INTEGRITY

We believe each competitor should be treated with the same courtesy and kindness, and that a judge should set a high standard of manners in the ring. To say good morning, smile, and to remember to thank each rider at the end of a show should be second nature, and a kind word goes a long way to setting the jockeys at ease. A quick eye to check that saddlery is safe, that girths are tight enough, and that all is correctly fitted, is a responsibility for all judges to be aware of, especially when judging smaller children.

It is not appropriate for a conformation judge to ask a competitor how he got on in the jumping phase. The best reply is 'Very well, thank you,' whatever happened. A conformation judge should not be influenced by performances in the jumping phase.

If a judge knows any of the competitors personally, he should treat them just the same as the other riders; it is not good form to greet a competitor or address one by name. Once a competitor is performing for a judge, he should watch the child until he has finished. The rider, for his part, should salute the judge on completion of his performance – it is very rude to sail straight out of the ring.

USING THE MARKS – JUMPING PHASE

Marking for manners can begin as soon as a pony enters the ring. If he trots in purposefully, halts a little away from the judge, obediently waiting to be told he may start, this makes a good beginning. A salute and 'Good morning' from the jockey completes the preliminaries after giving his number to the marking steward. This is ringcraft and good manners, and should be recognised by the judge as such, and all things being equal, this competitor deserves an extra mark over the badly presented pony.

During the jumping round the judge is looking for fluency, control, and an intelligent approach to the course as a whole. If the course is well built the pony will meet his fences correctly and jump with a smooth parabola. If not, he may cat jump and meet his fences on the wrong stride. A jockey who can see a stride and put his pony correctly at a fence in these circumstances deserves extra marks. He will have walked the course and watched other competitors, will have noticed any difficulties and will be ready to jump the course fluently. This amount of care should not go unnoticed or unrewarded by the judge and he should not be afraid to use the whole spectrum of marks, from 10 down to zero if necessary, to differentiate the good, the indifferent, and the poor.

Stops and knockdowns have their own penalties, and marks for manners should not be deducted as well unless the pony naps, bucks, rears, or exhibits any other resistances not related to the actual jumping.

USING THE MARKS – SHOWING PHASE

When the competition develops to the showing stage, again manners and production are of paramount importance. An ordinary pony should be able to collect very high marks for an excellent show in spite of being given rather low marks for conformation. Also there is no reason why this pony should not be beautifully mannered. So it is up to the judge to be fair, giving marks where they are due, or, even giving none if a pony is very naughty.

During the in-hand stage where the conformation of the pony is being judged, good presentation will help any pony to attain extra marks; conversely, standing up a good pony badly will certainly not help him to maximise on his performance. An experienced judge will be able to see through these problems and ask the good pony to be stood up correctly. Here is an opportunity for him to help the less-experienced jockey by showing him how to stand the pony correctly. Sometimes the jockey is very nervous and just needs a kind person in the ring to show him what to do.

A pony with a blemish should be very carefully assessed in terms of whether the blemish is a result of trauma or breakdown. Looking at the conformation should help him in this decision, because bad conformation is often the cause of breakdown. The position of the blemish will also help in this decision. On equal marks, a pony that is unblemished must go above a blemished one.

Having finished all the marking the judge is responsible for the correct totalling of the marks, and the figures must be checked. If there are any ponies on equal marks, the totals must be double-checked. If the addition is correct then the ponies' attributes must be considered again, taking into account how the marks are allotted. To separate three such ponies and having decided on their final order, the easiest solution is to award one a plus, leaving one at the original score and give the other a minus (e.g. 86+, 86, 86−). In this way, the other competitors' marks do not need to be altered up or down and the result is easily understood by the riders when they look at the marks after the class.

It is important to use all the marks available, otherwise the result will be lots of ponies having the same mark. Most people know when their pony has done well or badly, and know what to expect. Judges who use the marks well are respected for doing so.

JUDGING MIXED HEIGHT NOVICE CLASSES

The most difficult class to judge is the mixed height novice class, and this is where a singlehanded judge has the advantage. He can assess the quality of the ponies during the jumping phase and mark accordingly during phase two. Many a pony will receive a higher mark in his novice class than he will in an open class later in the day. Novice classes are for encouragement so his mark could go from 25 in the novice to 21 in the open. These marks are relative only to the class to which they refer, and a conformation mark is not an absolute mark, just a mark relative to the other ponies in that particular class. Some judges mark low and some high, and nobody would wish to give a novice a very low mark because newcomers should be encouraged to enjoy their classes and to try and improve. With training, feeding and time, the 21-mark novice can improve and mature to the 25 mark after a year or two.

JUDGING INSIDE THE RING

It may be interesting to the competitor to look at a show from a judges' point of view as this may explain some of the problems which may and do occur. As soon as a judge has been invited to judge at a show his first obligation is to reply as quickly as possible, and discover the number and type of classes. Each judge knows how many classes he or she can judge before losing concentration so the distance to be travelled to the show must be weighed against the time expected to be actually judging. On looking through the schedule you will find that WHP judges are expected to judge more classes than most, e.g. possibly three novices, a cradle stakes and nursery stakes, three opens and a championship! This can take seven to eight hours if done properly. Yet hacks, show pony and hunter judges would usually be expected only to judge three or four classes. This may well explain why so many show secretaries say they cannot find a judge for their show. Whoever invites the judge to the show should discuss with him how many classes he can cope with, and whether he prefers to judge alone or with another. Unless judges are asked about these things a show could either find itself with two judges unnecessarily, or one struggling for too long.

Having accepted to judge, it is a good idea to check there will be a BSPS coursebuilder, a good collecting-ring steward, and some help available to replace knocked-down fences. Very often a show will be very happy for you to bring a companion who will be able to help as a steward.

It is always a bonus to have a BSPS coursebuilder because they understand the working pony's way of going. If you have another coursebuilder, you may have to be very tactful in getting the course right for the class. It is ultimately the responsibility of the judge to be sure the course is safe and correct in height. The size of the ring and the going on the day will dictate the type of course in terms of height, related distances, and the position of the fences in the ring.

Novices need ground-lines wherever possible, simple fences with fillers, not more than one parallel, and a very carefully placed double so that they will jump with comfort and confidence. They are still learning and gaining experience and cannot cope with complicated courses. For the open ponies the coursebuilder has more freedom but he must keep within the maximum heights as these are for championship shows only.

Having accepted an invitation one needs to plan ahead and work out how long you will be away from home; certainly, you have to be on the showground for longer than most competitors. Once a competitor has been judged he can go home, but a judge stays until all the classes have finished, signs any forms, etc. before heading for home.

A judge must be well turned out: he is an ambassador of the BSPS. The weather at 6 a.m. is not always a good indicator of what the next twelve hours will be like, so take a range of clothing to cater for all conceivable sorts of weather. Wearing several layers can sometimes be the answer, then they can be peeled off if the day warms up.

A judge must be fully aware of all the rules, and there are many; but always have a rule book handy in case of problems.

When all is said and done, a judge can only please one person in each class, and that is the winner. However, if the rest of the class feel they have been fairly judged, and are placed roughly where they expected, then most people will be content. And if they have learned something from their day out, so much the better.

JUDGING OUTSIDE THE RING

Whenever you go to a show, whether as a spectator or an exhibitor, inevitably you will also be judging the classes, if only from the ringside. Armed with a catalogue and a few friends to chatter to, you are in a unique position to form a general opinion of all the exhibitors in the ring. A most useful exercise for a spectator is to assess the type of animal and performance that the judge is looking for in a particular class, with a view to buying a pony for a child to ride. This is time well spent, and helps you form a clearer idea of pony types. Study the catalogue, talk to people who have competed successfully for a number of years, and make notes discreetly. It will stand you in good stead when you come to buying or selling.

If you are watching a class in which you have an exhibit, do try to be objective and not stable blind. Look hard at the opposition, work out what their good points are, then look at your own combination and find as many faults as you can. You can then go home and work constructively for future improvement and success.

Always greet your jockey cheerfully when he comes out of the ring; if he has not done well, he will be feeling this already. Later on, when the team has had time to relax, you can get together in a constructive atmosphere to discuss future strategy. However young the child, always listen to his point of view and give him room to think for himself; this will help him to respect your views and to improve next time he is in the ring.

Above all, do not criticise him in front of other people, nor should you criticise other exhibitors. There is nothing wrong in discussing someone's performance in private so long as it is a way of explaining how something went wrong. Also, try not to criticise the judge; a competent judge will not have seen a catalogue and he will judge the exhibits before him as they are on that day and not on their previous or alleged record. He may still be working in that show ring many hours after you have gone home.

JUDGING FROM THE COMPETITOR'S POINT OF VIEW

Once a competitor is in the ring he should stop worrying whether he believes this particular judge likes him or his pony, and concentrate on making the best of the opportunity he has. Never forget that if a pony goes well he cannot be ignored; every entrant is bound to be looked at – after all, each pony jumps individually and will probably be seen in company with the rest of the class. A rider who does a good job will almost certainly earn reasonable marks. Very often only a few points separate the first few competitors in a class, so a few extra marks picked up here and there for a good performance could make all the difference.

TRAINING OF JUDGES

Nowadays most societies have some workable scheme to produce competent judges for their panels and the BSPS has been very forward-looking in this respect. Several years ago if one wished to become a judge the opportunity was provided to go into the show ring with some ponies and to later describe on paper and in interview one's appraisal of the exhibits. This was successful to a degree but presented a daunting prospect for anyone who was knowledgeable but shy, so only a small proportion of candidates were invited to be on the panel using this system.

The next system seemed to work better. The area committees recommended prospective candidates to the BSPS and if considered to have sufficient knowledge and background, these were asked to become probationary judges for a year. It was up to these probationers to arrange to judge with experienced judges at least four affiliated shows during the season. They had to approach judges who didn't know them, try to judge away from home and ask these judges to report to the BSPS after their day out together.

This system could tell the BSPS a great deal about a person's ability in the ring. It also gave them some idea how they would dress in the ring, whether they knew the rules, and whether they came prepared, on time, were discreet and courteous. This gave a 'judge-to-be' a wonderful opportunity to get used to working in the ring, and, if they were lucky, a gift of knowledge from half a dozen dedicated judges.

The latest method of selecting judges is for candidates to go forward for appraisal at a special conference day. Here ponies are produced, and future judges have the opportunity to judge them with experienced judges in attendance. If at this stage they are considered satisfactory, they are invited to complete a probationary year. Reports are sent back to the BSPS on how these probationary judges perform, and they are assessed as to whether they go forward on to the panel.

TYPES OF JUDGE

Someone who makes a good show pony judge does not necessarily make a good hunter-type judge. The former is usually an expert on conformation, but he must also judge for type. Up until 1978 there were two panels of judges: one for show ponies and one for working hunter ponies. All show pony judges were allowed to judge WHP classes but WHP judges were confined to WHPs. Many show pony judges did not have experience with WHPs and consequently the finer pony was put up in favour of the hunter type. This tended to make WHPs feel like second-class citizens. It was quite right, however, that WHP judges were not allowed to judge show ponies, unless they were experienced, conversant with the type, and on the show pony panel. Later, new judges' lists were produced: one for show ponies, one for WHPs and one for both types. This was a move in the right direction, but the notion that any judge who is right for show ponies is right for WHPs was really not adequate. Now judges are beginning to accept the true hunter type as a type in his own right.

The latest judges' list works very well. There is now only one list, but by the side of each name are letters indicating which classes he or she is allowed to judge. These are S for show ponies; H for show hunter ponies; and W for working hunter ponies.

RESPONSIBILITIES OF THE JUDGE

One of the responsibilities of a judge is to be sure that the show complies with the requirements of the BSPS. This is a sticky problem but if the show's facilities are inadequate this is not fair on the competitors. One of the most problematical areas is the size and terrain of the show rings. Show ponies require large flat rings, and although a jumping ring may be undulating or rough, the conformation ring should be as flat as possible. The recommended ring size is 100 yds/m by 60 yds/m, since anything smaller makes galloping difficult.

Another responsibility of the judge is to ensure that there is no cruelty to the ponies in the classes he is judging. If he finds this to be the case he must have the courage to report the incident to the show secretary, and to the BSPS.

CONCLUSIONS ON JUDGING

The judge must take full responsibility for the classes he is judging. He has to be at the show in good time, check the course if it is a WHP class, make sure the marker knows how to fill in the marksheet, check the marks at the end, know the rules inside out, be polite and courteous all day long, judge as fairly in the morning as in the afternoon, and check the safety of all the children and their tack.

He has to be strong enough to insist that things are put right if they are wrong. He has rules to work to, and some shows are not up to scratch. If rules are flouted and classes go ahead, they could, in theory, be declared null and void. If a show refuses to comply with the rules, the judge has to decide whether to refuse to judge or even write a disclaimer for the show before he starts to judge. With children one cannot be too safety conscious.

The judge has to be in full control, and if he is on his toes the show will run more smoothly. He must be aware of how much time is allotted to his classes so as not to make the show run behind schedule; this is particularly important if another judge needs to come into the ring after he has finished. He must be well turned out and prepared for all weathers, have a measuring stick, marking board, pencil rubber, whistle, rule book, a good road map and a watch.

He will need to be decisive so that he can judge fluently and consistently. He will need to be able to instruct stewards and jockeys on how he wishes to judge so that everyone knows how they stand and what to do. As far as the children are concerned, he must be kind, encouraging, and attentive throughout each show. If time is short, then he must watch the same amount of each jockey's show, so that they know he is being fair.

When it comes to stripping, the time available and the type of show will dictate how many to strip or whether to strip at all. A qualifier should always include stripping, if not all the ponies, a fair number, and the same number in each class. If there is a championship, he must be sure that the fences are the same for all the classes included in the championship.

The course could pose some problems, so it is important to walk it, measure it, consider the related distances, and consider the fences in relation to the terrain and the going. Any obstacle that could be in the way if a child falls off, must be removed. He should talk to the coursebuilder and have his co-operation.

A judge should thank all the people who help to make this day a happy one. *Above all, the judge should look for the correct type of pony that the class designates is being judged.*

CHAPTER 13

Coursebuilding

THE COURSE

A working hunter course is different from a show-jumping track, the most obvious difference being the colour of the jumps and their furnishing. It is clearly much more appropriate to test a hunter over the type of fence he is likely to meet out hunting, and, within reason, the more we can simulate these conditions in the ring the better. So rustic poles, unpainted wings and plenty of greenery in the form of branches etc. are the order of the day. But this is not the only difference, nor indeed the most important consideration a coursebuilder has to bear in mind.

Firstly, unlike in show-jumping, a coursebuilder is not trying to achieve a result with his course; the jumping is only a part of the overall assessment of the judge. Manners, way of going, conformation, type, also have a part to play in deciding the winner.

The course must look solid, since solid fences encourage clean jumping. Also they should not collapse at the slightest rattle.

One of the most important considerations is the relative position of the obstacles. The aim is not to find the best acrobat who can check and turn before each jump with skill and precision, rather the pony who will take his rider across country all day with the maximum of ease, comfort, and safety. Jumps must be so positioned as to encourage smooth jumping at a steady hunting pace.

With a hunter course, height is not the main criterion. A longer bascule is required, to cope with an unexpected back pole or back ditch. The hunter pony must be able to take these things in his stride.

A showground with undulations and interesting features such as banks, ditches, hedges, etc., offers a hunter coursebuilder opportunities which would be inappropriate for show-jumping.

The BSPS offer advice to show organisers, both in their rule book and in their coursebuilder's guide, a booklet which they published in 1982. Anyone intending to put on a show or build courses should study these publications.

SAFETY

There is some element of risk in most sports, but it is sensible to keep it to a minimum. There is no sense in creating obstacles which incorporate features known to increase the danger. Obstacles should be capable of being knocked down; so fixed, event-type jumps are undesirable.

Spread fences, like parallels with depth, should have a single pole only at the back, and this pole must not be below the height of the top pole at the front.

Wings should have no sharp bolts protruding, and are best erected with the smooth head of any bolts facing the approaching rider, any screw protruding through the nuts should be cut off with a hacksaw and filed smooth. The sharp ends of pins securing the cups on the wings should be at the rear of the jump.

'Blind' bounces can be dangerous, e.g. a 'bullfinch' into a jump at a bounce distance, because a bold jumper can land almost on top of the back fence and go head-over-heels.

Gates, planks and other uprights should be rested on flat cups, not the deep cups used to support poles. Gates must swing freely

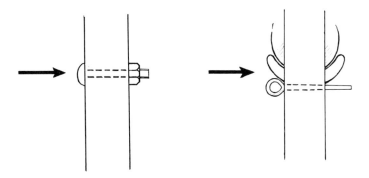

Fig. 13.1 Jump fittings. (a) Nuts in wings – protruding bolts should be cut off and filed, and the smooth head of the bolt should face the approaching rider. (b) The sharp ends of cup pins should be at the rear of the jump.

on their cups and must not rest sloping on the ground.

Straw bales can cause problems if their twine gets caught by a pony's foot, perhaps getting hooked on a loose shoe or protruding nail. If a coursebuilder is short of fillers, bales are sometimes used, but they are better used with a pole or poles above them so that they are jumped clear.

One dangerous practice is building a fence so that the pony lands on rising ground behind it. This puts extra strain on the forelegs, and frequently causes the pony to 'peck' on landing, since the legs have not had time to unfold at the knee. The opposite, ground falling away on landing is, within reason, safer and a good test.

The going must be taken into consideration; jumping downhill on a very slippery surface, especially a combination, can cause a lot of falls.

The coursebuilder must get his course right before the class starts; once someone has jumped it cannot be changed because every competitor must compete over the same course. If some feature is causing a lot of dangerous incidents, the judge must decide whether to proceed or cancel the class on safety grounds. Whatever he does, he will be criticised, but in time his wisdom may be appreciated.

Parents should withdraw their child from a class if they are unhappy about the safety of the course. At the same time they should complain to the show secretary in writing. In a case of alleged negligence they should also complain in writing to the BSPS office and ask another member parent to back them up. This other parent must have a pony competing in the same class.

COURSEBUILDING

If you are invited to build a course it is as well to ask a few questions before you accept for you will need to define the extent of your responsibilities.

Will you be expected to provide the jumps and deliver and remove them after the show? If the show is providing the jumps, are they rustic? How many wings are available; how many poles; can they send you a list of the materials they have?

How many classes are there and in how many rings? Are the classes affiliated to the BSPS? What time of day do the classes commence? Will you need to build the day before? Will you be

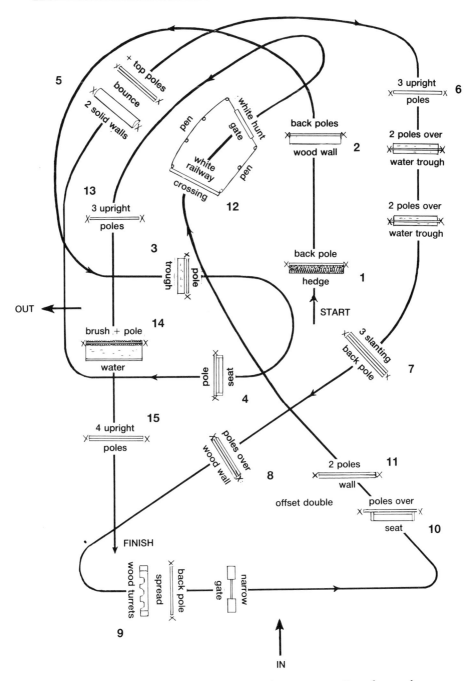

Fig. 13.2 The 1981 BSPS Open Championship course at Peterborough, comprising twenty fences in all.

(TOP) *Wooden wall with back pole, Peterborough.* (ABOVE) *Seat with back pole, Peterborough.* (Photos: *J. Thorne*)

expected to dismantle afterwards, and load jumps? What help can be provided? Will you be expected to bring an assistant?

Is the show indoors or outside? If indoors, what is the exact dimension of the school?

If you charge a fee or expenses then this should be made clear at this stage – small shows will have limited funds. Put it in writing.

You will probably be interested to know who is judging the

(TOP) *Bounce fence of two rounded walls of wood, Peterborough.* (ABOVE) *First part of off-set double, Peterborough.* (Photos: *J. Thorne*)

jumping phase.

If you accept the job, your ability as a coursebuilder will be judged by all at the ringside, and it is very frustrating to arrive at a show to find totally inadequate materials and no assistance. So it is a good idea to write a very clear letter of acceptance to the organisers, setting out what has been agreed between you and listing your own needs. You may well be able to influence the show at this stage by laying the foundations for a good course,

(TOP) *First part of a pen-type fence, Peterborough.* (ABOVE) *Two upright poles over foliage, Peterborough.* (Photos: *J. Thorne*)

e.g. you could remind them how big the ring needs to be and that it doesn't have to be a particularly flat ring, as long as there is a good place to gallop – this may give the organisers more scope for siting the ring.

The order in which the classes run can help you too. It is easier to reduce the sizes of jumps than to increase them; this applies to the three open, three novice, and three restricted classes. If you build a good flowing course for the big ones, the little ones have

(TOP) *Slanting hedge with back pole and water, Peterborough.* (ABOVE) *Double fence of wooden wall into a spread, Peterborough.* (Photos: *J. Thorne*)

no problems, but the converse is not necessarily true.

Ask to have a schedule sent to you as soon as it is printed.

Remind the organisers that you will need a couple of strong helpers to position the jumps, some young people to help rebuild any fences knocked down during the classes, and, most important, help with dismantling afterwards if this is your responsibility. You will be tired by then and keen to go home. You cannot automatically expect this help unless you ask for it beforehand.

About three weeks before the show, phone your contact and enquire how the arrangements for your requirements are proceeding, small shows sometimes forget and leave things to the last minute.

If you live fairly near the showground but do not know the site, it is useful to look at the ground beforehand; otherwise arrive an hour beforehand on the day you are building. Decide in your mind where all the jumps will be (or better still, do a rough sketch), and note what changes you propose to make for the different classes. If you have cradle and nursery stakes, three open classes, three heights of novices, and associates, that makes nine different set-ups (and that is without restricted classes, and open working hunter, which they sometimes ask you to 'pull in'). If there are only half a dozen entries in each class you could spend all day rebuilding your course.

You will require a small amount of kit. The first essentials are a rule for measuring heights and spreads of fences, and a rule book to refer to. If you do the job regularly it is useful to make your own rule out of a hardwood lath, with various heights and spreads for different classes marked on it. If it is 6 ft (180 cm) long then it can also be used for the separation distances of doubles and other combinations. Some baler twine, a few tools, like a hand axe, bow saw, secateurs, a hammer, and a few nails, etc., will also come in handy. You will need plenty of clothing to cope with all sorts of weather.

When planning the course, make the first few jumps relatively easy to enable the competitors to establish a good rhythm before facing the more challenging obstacles which will be required to sort out the ponies.

Remember:

(a) ascending fences are easier than upright ones or parallels;
(b) fences with ground-lines are easier than those with gaps at the bottom;
(c) wide fences are easier than narrow ones like stiles – 15 ft (4.5 m) is a good width but only if the poles are light, e.g. birchwood;
(d) on a slight incline it is easier to jump uphill rather than downhill;
(e) fences jumped towards the collecting ring are easier than those jumped away from it;
(f) it is easier to jump across or away from low bright sun than

towards it, especially with dew on the ground;

(g) fences with ditches in front are more difficult than plain fences;

(h) jumping out of bright conditions into darkness, e.g. woodland, is very testing;

(i) walking or trotting through water will always cause problems with a large number of ponies;

(j) doubles, whose first element is a parallel, are more difficult than an upright followed by a parallel;

(k) anything that distracts a pony as he approaches a fence will cause difficulties (at one area show a ditch was dug and the spoil was put in two piles either side of the approach to the jump – it caused absolute havoc);

(l) sharp turns into or between fences, e.g. off the side of the ring, are difficult;

(m) any series of fences in quick succession requires great skill and concentration;

(n) any fence following closely after a difficult one is frequently knocked down;

(o) combinations with incorrect spacing will cause problems and jerky jumping, especially with larger ponies.

It is not clever to make a course too difficult; what is clever is getting it just right so that:

(a) no-one is eliminated (except those who were not ready to compete);

(b) no rider is frightened and put off from trying again;

(c) there is a limited number of refusals;

(d) there are no pony falls (definitely none going head-over-heels);

(e) there are no rider falls – bad with any child but inexcusable in the cradle and nursery stakes;

(f) there are enough knockdowns so that there are not too many clear rounds;

(g) there are no long delays whilst complicated 'bogey' fences have to be rebuilt;

(h) no obstacle invites prolonged disobedience, such as a shallow river which has to be crossed by wading;

(i) no pony is put off jumping forever after experiencing fear.

If you are short of materials then white wings can be used but they must be well furnished with green branches etc. Another way of using materials economically is to include one fence which can be jumped from both directions, or even the same way with a different approach. But if you do this the fence must be simple and quick to re-erect so as not to hold up a competitor making his second approach. Include several jumps in between to give you more time.

Whenever a fence is demolished, it is vital that it is rebuilt exactly as it was. Unless you can remember the dimensions of every fence have a few quick notes handy. Do not rebuild while a pony is jumping unless the fence is to be jumped again by the same pony.

The course you build should depend on the nature of the show and the standard and number of entries. It is a good rule to build easier courses earlier in the season, and gradually increase the difficulty towards the championships (however, this should not apply to the Royal International qualifiers which are early in the season).

It is quite in order for a coursebuilder to consult the catalogue to assess the entry, to help decide on the standard of the course. Catalogues should not, of course, be taken into the ring, nor should the entries be discussed with the judge.

It is recommended that all the courses at an event which includes a championship be built as near as possible the same, except for height and spread. Judges are asked to use WHP marks as a guide in championships, so however even the marking is in other respects, if the course is different, then this could affect the result of a championship. Bear in mind that ditches must not be dug too wide so as to exceed the spread of 13-handers; gates must not be so high that they will not swing freely on the cups in the 13-hh classes – two gates, one for the 14 hh and 15 hh classes, and a lower one, otherwise identical, for the 13 hh class, are ideal.

When you have finished building, walk round the course imagining how you would jump it, and put a number on each fence and combination.

BUILDING INDOORS

This is a more precise occupation and since many indoor events are for novices, it is important to get these courses right. From a coursebuilder's point of view, putting off novices with unsuitable courses is almost as deadly a sin as unnerving small children.

Your course should be constructed so that it can be ridden in big sweeping curves with no sharp twists and turns, and because space is so restricted indoors, there will be a tendency to put the fences near the centre of the arena. Some builders draw a scale diagram of the school, and show not only the jumps but also the route which the ponies are expected to take.

On the day, make yourself known to the judge and offer to walk the course with him. Explain why you have built it as you have and ask his opinion on any question at all controversial; listen to his views. If you do this, he is less likely to want to rebuild your course.

The judge is ultimately responsible for safety and for complying with the rules, but he should not spoil your course for the sake of a fad. However, most judges are perfectly reasonable and understanding. You will be judged solely on the course you build – if the course does not jump well, you will be blamed.

Finally, although you should be available at the ringside, you are best out of the ring during the actual jumping. Never interfere with a competitor who is jumping except perhaps to catch a pony, help someone remount, or if someone is injured.

CHAPTER 14

Organisations

ENGLAND, SCOTLAND AND WALES

THE BRITISH SHOW PONY SOCIETY

The BSPS is the largest society in Britain catering for ridden show ponies, hunter ponies and working hunter ponies. Their championships held each September are the biggest ridden pony show in the world. The BSPS is a democratic society run by a council who are elected by the adult members.

Within the council there are many and various sub-committees which deal with the differing activities of the society. There is a championship show committee, a winter championship committee and other committees for team selection, conference organisation, publicity promotions and fund-raising, executive and finance, qualifying shows and judges' assessment. Judges are appointed and reappointed annually, each case being considered individually. New judges are appointed by the council on the recommendation of the assessment committee, who hold assessment days and receive reports on candidates from senior judges with whom the latter have worked as probationers. The whole country is divided into area branches, which have their own committees, individual AGMs and put on area shows. Sometimes they arrange team competitions against other areas. Most areas hold shows in both the winter and summer, and each area is responsible for its own solvency, receiving no money from head office. Area chairmen hold occasional meetings, which provide an important forum for discussing grass-root opinions. Each year area chairmen elect a chairman from amongst their number, and this person is normally co-opted on to the council.

Organisation

This is done from a central office, with a full-time secretary and several full and part-time helpers. All the checking of schedules for affiliated shows is done here, as is record-keeping for membership, judges, and pony registrations. A monthly review with news, interesting dates and show results is published from the central office and distributed to members.

Rules

These are most comprehensive. A new book is issued yearly and should be read carefully. Showing members are responsible for being aware of the rules, which change slightly every year.

Complaints

If there are any problems or complaints concerning members, ponies, judges, producers, or shows, these should be made in writing to the secretary of the BSPS and preferably backed up by a second member. The person who is the subject of the complaint is given the opportunity to state his or her point of view. The council then considers the evidence impartially and decides on further action. They may conclude the matter, or pass it to a disciplinary committee. Serious complaints may be referred to the steward of the society, who may hold an enquiry if necessary.

Participation

On joining the BSPS it is a good idea to become familiar with your area organisation. They arrange many interesting functions and these afford an excellent way of getting to know people. The names of area chairmen are printed in the rule book.

Wales, although part of the BSPS, is an independent area and, as such, may make up both area and national teams for competition against other areas and nations. Scotland has a separate branch and officers but is bound by the same BSPS constitution and rules. Scotland works closely with England and Wales and has a representative on the council.

The address of the BSPS is: 124 Green End Road, Sawtry, Huntingdon, Cambridgeshire; chairman: Mrs J. Gibson, MFH; Secretary: Mrs J. Toynton.

IRELAND

THE IRISH PONY SOCIETY

The Irish Pony Society governs the showing of ponies in the whole of Ireland. Their marking system is quite different from ours in that ponies are expected to do all their work in a peaceful mannerly way, but preferably in snaffle bridles with no gadgets at all. The courses are not so high as ours, nor so difficult. Each fence is judged individually with more marks allocated to a well-mannered round with knock-downs, than to a sticky or over-enthusiastic clear. With this in mind a pony jumping a round sweetly but with a few faults can expect to beat a rapid and unbalanced clear. This attitude encourages breeders to produce ponies of the shape and temperament to jump freely and steadily, and trainers to spend time in producing ponies that are obedient and balanced.

The Irish seem prepared to spend more time on training their ponies, although they have fewer opportunities to show them. In Britain, no sooner is one season finished, than we immediately plunge ourselves into the next, and with an overriding drive to qualify. The Irish, however, do not have the same sense of urgency, because they do not have so many opportunities.

Rules

Low, inviting courses are specified, designed to encourage good, free jumping, with the pony using itself in the correct style over its fences. The pony must be suitable for the child who is riding it. It should have a steady head carriage with no resistance to the rider's hand, have sufficient impulsion, yet be balanced and rhythmical throughout the course. An even canter should be maintained where at all possible as a break in the pace spoils the fluency of the round. Excessive speed is neither required nor desirable. A clear round in poor style will not be likely to feature in the second phase. Snaffle bridles are encouraged (and gain a bonus mark in novice classes); martingales are not; drop nosebands are acceptable. Boots may be worn in the jumping phase to protect the pony's legs.

Ponies should be schooled to gallop on when asked, but should be under control at all times. They must be taught to lead freely in hand and stand up correctly for the judge. The pony should be a well-made quality type with more substance than a show pony, and a free mover, capable of galloping on. Ponies should be inspected as in other show classes for type, conformation, quality and substance, as applicable to hunter ponies. Throughout, the emphasis is on performance and manners.

Novice courses must have a minimum of six fences and may not include a double or water, but open classes must have a minimum of eight fences, a change of direction, spreads, correctly spaced doubles, and water if possible. The judge is entirely responsible for the course and must check it before commencing to judge. He or she puts symbols on the score sheets to explain the marks given for each fence.

Marking – phase 1 The jumping is rather complicated because, although 60 per cent of the total marks are allocated here, there will be a minimum of eight fences in the open classes, each carrying a maximum of 10 marks, from 10 for excellent, to 1 for bad. A first refusal is 10 faults, a second is 20 faults, but if then a pony jumps a fence after a refusal, he is judged as if it were his first attempt, but having been penalised already. A knock-down has either 5 or 10 marks according to the severity of the knock; a fall of pony or rider is 20 faults.

Marking – phase 2 This phase is judged on manners in company, conformation, quality, movement and soundness, and is sometimes split into two phases. It is judged first collectively at the walk, trot and canter, and a brief individual show is performed. This show should include a circle at the trot on both reins, a figure-of-eight at the canter, a gallop, and a halt. Special attention is then given to conformation and type. Quality, movement, substance, and soundness are most important so this latter phase is carried out in-hand.

Irish ponies are awarded points, and having gained a certain number in novice classes are deemed to be classified as open ponies. Novice ponies are not encouraged to enter open classes. Points for each pony are recorded by the Irish Pony Society. Stallions are sometimes allowed to compete, and JA ponies may compete in open classes.

The Irish way of judging hunter ponies has a lot to offer, and we in Britain would do well to emulate many of their attitudes.

PONIES ASSOCIATION (UK) (ex The Ponies of Britain)

This organisation is probably the most versatile society for ponies in Britain. It caters for a vast array of ponies and riders of all ages, covering all the indigenous breeds, show ponies, hunter ponies, working hunter ponies, both in-hand and ridden. They have at least four major shows each year, and many other shows affiliate to this society for their competitors to qualify for their various championships. Their main championship show is in August each year. They publish an annual and have their own panel of judges for the various sections.

The office is at 56 Green End Road, Sawtry, Huntingdon, Cambridgeshire; chairman: Mrs J. Lee-Smith.

THE NORTHERN COUNTIES PONY ASSOCIATION

This is a well-established organisation serving the needs of the Midlands and the north of England. All breeds are catered for, both ridden and in-hand, and their shows have a great variety of classes. The Association is divided into several branches, and an overall Supreme Championship for champions of champions is held at the close of the season for all the ponies who qualify. An interesting journal is produced each year with news of ponies and studs in the North. Honorary secretaries: Mr and Mrs Halliwell, Lees Hall Farm, Glossop, Derbys, SK13 9JT.

THE HUNTER PONY STUD BOOK REGISTER

This is a comparatively new register especially created for the registration of hunter ponies for breeding purposes. It was started because there was no other register for these ponies, which are a type in their own right. Entry into the register is by winning an in-hand or ridden class at open level, and gradually pedigrees will evolve as the register progresses. Many shows affiliate their classes to the HPSBR and at the end of the season supreme championships are held for the in-hand champions and reserve champions from these shows. The main objective of the register is to encourage breeders to breed ponies of hunter type, and the specifications are: correct conformation for riding and endurance; substance without coarseness; quality without fineness; straightness and freedom of action at all paces; natural balance; jumping ability and boldness; steady temperament, suitable for a child; size not to exceed 15.2 hh; any colour. In due course the register will develop into a stud book. The ponies are graded, and those that have won open working hunter pony classes are considered the ultimate to breed from. At present this applies to mares, but in the future it is hoped that open classes for WHP stallions will be available so that stallions can prove themselves to be both well behaved and have ability under saddle in the show ring.

The Hunter Pony Stud Book Register office is at Beacon Cottage Farm, Deans Lane, Woodhouse Eaves, nr. Loughborough, Leicestershire; chairman and secretary: Mrs. S. Thorne, NDD.

APPENDIX 1: BSPS WHP SUPREME CHAMPIONS

Year	Pony	Owner
No qualification needed		
1968	Beckfield Ben Hur	Mrs E. Barham
1969	Beckfield Ben Hur	Mrs E. Barham
1970	Tonto	Mrs Clapham
1st and 2nd qualified at shows		
1971	Tonto	Mrs Clapham
1972	Beckfield Ben Hur	Mrs E. Barham
1st placed at shows to qualify		
1973	Lemington Carello	Mrs O'Neill
1974	Van de Valk	Mr & Mrs Massarella
1975	Caelow Planet	Mr & Mrs Lord
1976	Coalport	Mr & Mrs Crofts
1977	Rookery Jigsaw	Mrs Flack
1978	Lynscott Medallion	Mr & Mrs Brown
1979	Toyd Bewildered	Mr & Mrs Hunnable
1980	Twyford Cracker	Mrs Jackson
1981	Sefton Tony of Alderbourne	Mr Connor
1982	Nutbeam Minto	Mrs Dyson
1983	Nutbeam Minto	Mrs Dyson
1984	Just Jasper	Mrs King
1985	Little Diamond	Mr & Mrs Harrison
1986	Sandman	Mr Connor
1987	Towy Valley Maurice	Dr Micallef
1988	Something Original	Mr & Mrs Atkinson

APPENDIX 2: FURTHER READING

ARCHER HOUBLON, DOREEN, *Side-Saddle*, J.A. Allen, London, 1938 (revised edition 1973).

FITZWYGRAM, LT-GENERAL SIR F., *Horses and Stables*, Longmans, 1869.

HARRIS, CHARLES, *Fundamentals of Riding*, J.A. Allen, London, 1985.

HAYES, CAPT. HORACE, FRCVS, *Veterinary Notes for Horse Owners*, revised by J.F. Donald, Stanley Paul, London, 1968.

SMYTHE, R.H., MRCVS, *The Mind of the Horse*, J.A. Allen, London, 1965.

SUMMERHAYS, R.S., *The Problem Horse*, J.A. Allen, London, 1975.

WYNMALEN, H., *Equitation*, J.A. Allen, London, 1971.

INDEX